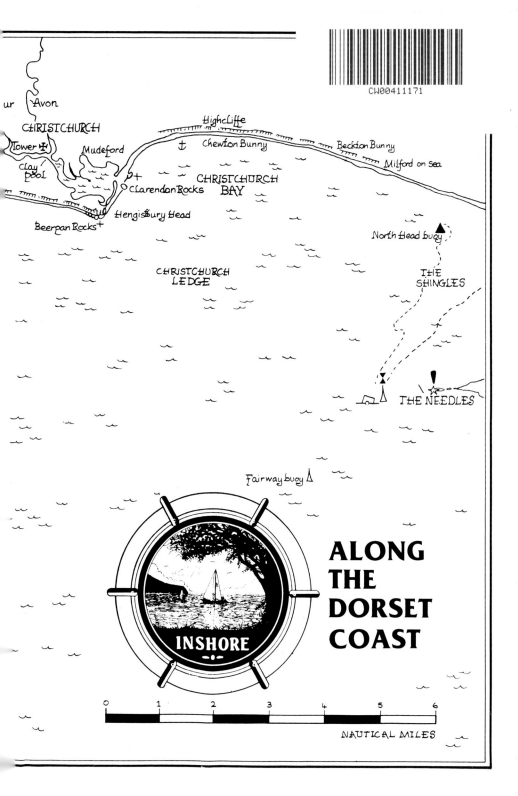

ur Avon

CHRISTCHURCH

Tower ⚓

Mudeford

Clay Pool

HighCliffe

⚓ Chewton Bunny

Beckton Bunny

Milford on Sea

Clarendon Rocks

CHRISTCHURCH BAY

Hengistbury Head

Beerpan Rocks

North Head buoy

CHRISTCHURCH LEDGE

THE SHINGLES

THE NEEDLES

Fairway buoy

ALONG THE DORSET COAST

INSHORE

| 0 | 1 | 2 | 3 | 4 | 5 | 6 |

NAUTICAL MILES

CW00411171

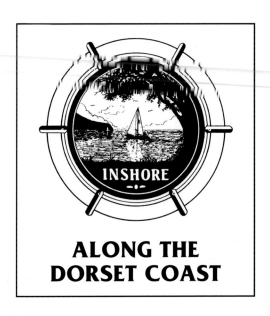

ALONG THE DORSET COAST

By PETER BRUCE

FIRST EDITION PUBLISHED MAY 1989
REPRINTED JUNE 1991
SECOND EDITION PUBLISHED APRIL 1996

Other pilotage books by the same author:
Solent Hazards
Solent Tides
Wight Hazards

Boldre Marine
Kestrel Cottage, Shirley Holms, Lymington,
Hampshire, SO41 8NH.
Tel & Fax (01590)683106

Contents

Acknowledgement

During my researches along the Dorset coast I have been fortunate to come across some wonderfully gifted and good people who have not only freely given much valuable information, but also passed me on to others of their own calibre. I should also thank those who have been kind enough to read the draft script. Their suggestions have been invaluable.

Caution

While every care has been taken in compiling this book, it is regretted that no responsibility can be taken by the author or publisher for inaccuracies or omissions, or for any accidents or mishaps resulting from its use.

Page layout by *Dragonfly*, 117 Portland Road, Bournemouth BH9 1NG.
Printed by Bookbuilders, Hong Kong

Front cover: Mupe Bay in August.
Back cover: East Worbarrow Bay at sunset.

Introduction

From the mariner's point of view enjoyment of the lovely east Dorset coast depends much upon the strength and direction of the wind. Perfection can occur when an area of high pressure sits benignly over the United Kingdom producing gentle northerly breezes. In these happy times one can get into tremendously attractive coves and anchorages along the south-facing coast between Anvil Point and Portland. The sea off this shore is much clearer than most places on the south coast, especially in settled weather, which means the seabed can be seen at depths of up to seven metres. This enables a spot to be picked for anchoring on sand rather than seaweed, which 'balls up' preventing the anchor from digging in. In addition the clear water helps one to pick the way through the rocks with confidence, thus making possible visits to more interesting places. Sunglasses, especially ones that polarise the light, can be most helpful. As a result of the good underwater visibility, sub-aqua diving operations are popular. They are identifiable by International Code flag 'A' on the diving tender, and a stream of air bubbles appearing on the surface from the divers themselves. Needless to say, divers are extremely vulnerable at or near the surface. Speaking of objects at or near the surface, it is worth recording that there are huge numbers of lobster pots laid between a point six miles south of St Aldhelm's (or St Alban's) Head and the equivalent point off Portland Bill.

There are sea danger areas associated with an Army range between St Aldhelm's Head and Lulworth, and the firing programme will often intrude upon coastal passage-making. At least we can be thankful that the personnel concerned are on our side! Information regarding the Lulworth range will be found in Chapter 12.

The detailed offshore research for this book was undertaken in a 9.9m yacht of 1.85m draught and an outboard-driven 4.5m launch of 0.5m draught, but anchorage and general information are given with vessels of up to two metres draught in mind. It is an area where larger vessels should take a dinghy, and when landing places are mentioned this applies to sailing dinghies, inflatable yacht tenders, and such craft as can normally take the beach in suitable conditions.

4

Plate 1. The Gadcliff.

Apart from the Shambles, there are few off-lying dangers in the area except for fierce tidal races, to be given due respect at spring tides. During strong onshore winds one should keep a good seven miles to seaward of the coast, which is well known for its tales of woe, though it can be said that most of these have occurred in winter. If conditions allow passage close inshore, the prudent mariner will consider where he should go to if it comes on to blow, in order to be ready to scuttle off to a safe port should the need arise. Of these, Poole Harbour has the added advantage of having a choice of delightful anchorages as well as marina berths.

The layout of the book takes the reader from east to west, starting from the Solent. The area covered extends from the Needles to Portland Bill, which many vessels can cover in one tide. If the weather is suitable on first setting out, it may be wise to go initially to the westward limit of the cruise area, so that exploration can be undertaken with, and not against, the prevailing wind.

Emphasis is given to information not obtainable in other nautical publications, but it is assumed that the local large scale charts and normal navigational data will be available. When planning voyages, time spent in reconnaissance on foot will seldom be wasted, and as a bonus there are few more beautiful cliff walks than on this coast.

Chapter 1

Christchurch Bay

The large open area of Christchurch Bay is, for most purposes, just a stretch of sea to be crossed. One approaches from the east by the Needles Channel, where one can cut the corner a little at the south-west Shingles Buoy, or from the North Channel where it is often possible to cross the North Head shoal rather than round North Head Buoy. At the other end of the bay pilotage is constrained by Christchurch Ledge which since 7 August 1988 for reasons of economy no longer has a navigational buoy, though a racing mark may be laid in roughly the same area during the summer.

The traditional lead for the experienced sailor in good visibility and fair weather across North Head is to keep Hurst Castle open its own width off Fort Victoria, the building overlooking Sconce Point. There are three metres on this line, with much the same 50m either side, but as the Shingles Bank is shifting continuously one should allow a good margin. When approaching the Solent from seaward in a south-westerly gale there is much to be said for using the North Channel, thus avoiding the steep breaking seas off the Needles.

Having much less tide than the Solent, Christchurch Bay is used from time to time in reasonable summer weather for yachting events such as Admiral's Cup inshore races. Racing craft will be identifiable by a flag on the backstay, and passage-makers will find it more comfortable to keep a sensible distance clear during these events to avoid being politely invited to do so

Plate 2. It is possible to land at Beckton Bunny either alongside the wall or in the corner of the cliff.

Plate 3. Chewton Bunny.

by a race official, or probably less politely so by a competitor. A sensible distance can be quite close if one is not in a competitor's way, on his wind or creating wash.

From between the two dragon's teeth on the cliff top at Taddiford Gap, once the site of a Roman encampment, at low water one can see on the beach the scanty remains of the 32m schooner *Lamorna*, wrecked about five years after World War II. She had suffered steering and engine failure, and had then been damaged whilst under tow. *Lamorna* was built of teak on steel frames. Her large curved keel fabrication lies just below the Gap, and other structural members, such as a shroud plate and a mast step, are on the beach a little further to the west.

Christchurch Bay beach is popular for bathing and windsurfing, but is too much of an unsheltered lee shore for yachts, except in settled offshore winds. In exceptionally calm weather a small boat can get alongside the sewer pipe bund at Beckton Bunny (Plate 2). There is not much to tie up to on the wall, but there is a pleasant shingly beach with access to the cliff top walk which extends from Keyhaven to Naish Farm beside Highcliffe. Alternatively, a small shallow bay will be found on the east side of the bund which gives a sheltered beach landing when the wind is from the west. The rocks forming the bay extend some way out from the bund, so approach should be from the east.

One can get up the cliff with ease at Beckton Bunny and Chewton Bunny (Plate 3), which made these landing sites favoured by smugglers in the 18th Century. Moreover, they were

7

Plate 4. The Run at Christchurch.

both mined for the same reason during the last world war. In climbing the cliffs, one should avoid any areas of soft mud from which over-adventurous people have been known to require extraction by the fire brigade. There is plenty of evidence of cliff erosion, and pill boxes in the sea probably indicate where the edge of the cliff was at the time of World War II. One of these pill boxes is about 100m west of Beckton Bunny sewer outfall, and, as it is covered at high water, could be a hazard to anyone landing by boat. Another pill box lies on the beach at Highcliffe. There may still be several tank traps hidden under the sand along this shore which can become exposed from time to time. For example the New Forest District Council had to remove a concrete and steel structure off a Hordle groyne which in 1995 was injuring swimmers.

If waiting for the tide there is an attractive anchorage by the wooded shore to the west of Highcliffe Castle, marked as 'bathing area' on the chart. The shingle and sand beach is steep, so one can get in quite close at high water. Though holding ground is supposed to be good offshore, it is not so good close in to the beach. There are no local anchoring restrictions and yachts can anchor off the entrance of Christchurch Harbour or anywhere else. Running parallel to this beach from Highcliffe to Hengistbury there are 14 yellow 'byelaw buoys', laid between

April and October, inshore of which speed is restricted to 8 knots. They are placed 350m apart, and 250m to seaward of the low water mark, except where it is necessary to site them clear of the Christchurch Harbour entrance marker buoys. This entrance is interesting in that it has seasonal variations from year to year. In winter the channel sometimes forms an extension of The Run off Mudeford Quay, heading north east. Then, during the spring, a new channel usually forms running eastwards (Plate 4). Of late the channel has varied greatly in position during the winter, but has settled in the usual easterly direction in the summer. Locally it is felt that the new groynes to the west of Hengistbury Head may have stabilised The Run after centuries of waywardness. For example it is believed that in prehistoric times The Run may have been west of Hengistbury, while in the 1880s it ran to the east as far as Highcliffe.

The Christchurch Harbour Association has the task of laying buoys appropriate to the inconstancies of the channel (Plate 5). In summer the most seaward buoys are a pair of conical and can shaped buoys on a black buoyancy chamber base, with round red and green channel buoys of about 0.6m diameter further in. Both the channel and the buoys are liable to shift in storms, and afterwards it may take a few days to sort things out. Yellow buoys are put out for the benefit of those who still go to sea in winter.

There is a stand in the tide of three to four hours at high water; so clearly the best time to enter, or leave, is on the first high tide. The channel is really very shallow, and limits general use to craft

Plate 5. The south end of The Run. The yacht has left the channel and appears to have gone aground.

Plate 6. Clay Pool, the confluence of the Stour and the Avon at Christchurch.

with a draught of 1.2m or less. It will be found that the well-marked channel gets deeper and prettier as one approaches Christchurch Priory. There is a T-junction at Clay Pool (Plate 6), giving a choice of going up the Avon or the Stour Rivers. The latter has more scope, allowing passage for sailing vessels up to Tuckton Bridge. This bridge, dating from 1905, was one of the earliest to be built in concrete and may need to be replaced before long. Though craft able to get under the bridge can theoretically navigate up to the tidal limit at Iford Bridge, one soon gets into private fishing country where visiting boats are not so welcome. Moreover the Blandford fly, with its vicious bite, is a force to be reckoned with between May and June. Nevertheless the lower mile of the Stour is worth a visit. There are attractive waterside houses to admire, and noisy Aylesbury ducks and self-drive hire

Plate 7. Mudeford lives up to its name.

Plate 8. Christchurch Harbour is generally shallow and the well-marked channels scarcely less so. The unmarked Clarendon Rocks can be seen in the foreground.

boats to contend with. The ordained tidal limit for the Avon is at Knapp Mill, opposite Christchurch Hospital and just beyond the railway bridge, not that anyone usually ventures that far. The best public launching sites, which are both free, are Mayor's Mead at The Quomps on the north side of the river Stour, or at Mudeford Quay (Plate 7), this latter site being, of course, much nearer to the sea. Smaller slipways, suitable only for dinghies, are on the opposite side of the river to Mayor's Mead, at Waterloo Bridge and at Stanpit.

The name Christchurch derives from a charming legend. The medieval builders of the priory had cut a beam short in the south choir aisle and it would not span the walls. The following day they were astonished to find that the same beam had mysteriously lengthened and now lay neatly in place. An unknown carpenter had been seen at the site and it was felt that such a miracle could only have been achieved if he had been Christ the Carpenter. Thus the building and the town became known as Christ's Church. The Priory, as it became in 1150, is a mixture of architectural styles from the Norman arches of the nave to the more delicate perpendicular style of the Great Quire and Lady Chapel, and is worth a visit.

The first obstacle to the south of the harbour entrance is Clarendon Rocks (Plate 8). This wall was built at the instigation of Lord Clarendon with the local stone, 'ironstone dogger', to be

11

the northerly mole of a new entrance to Christchurch Harbour. In hoping to make a major maritime port at Christchurch he was, no doubt, influenced by the fact that it used to be the chief port of iron age Britain. His project eventually started in 1692 with the construction of a new entrance and protective wall but was abandoned after the tremendous storm of 26 November 1703 which, amongst other things, caused the new entrance to be blocked. The unmarked 230m submerged wall remains as a notable handicap to inshore traffic. Although its position cannot be readily identified from coastal features, turbulence over it is often discernible.

There are three possibilities when rounding the dark-coloured Hengistbury Head. Small craft often hug the shore and pass very close to the stone groyne off the head to avoid Beerpan Rocks (Plate 9) and the shallow patch 0.2nm to the north-east. Alternatively, one can pass a mile or so offshore where a gap may be found in the awe inspiring breakers that appear when a sea is running onto Christchurch Ledge. There are large numbers of fishing floats on this rocky ledge and, in the absence of the navigational buoy, these may be the best indication of its outer limit which should be rounded if the inner routes do not seem wise. There is a coastguard lookout station on the headland used as a remote radio station for relaying radio signals by the Coastguard, which may be manned occasionally.

A large population lived on Hengistbury Head during the Bronze and Iron Ages and throughout the Roman occupation. At its western end was a double rampart and ditch, and the foundations of a Celtic fort remain on the promontory. Thousands of British coins, as well as continental pottery, have been unearthed which suggest considerable trading activity at the nearby port.

Plate 9. The Long Groyne at Hengistbury Head. Beerpan Rocks lurk in the seaweed.

Chapter 2

Poole Bay

Seafarers usually cross Poole Bay some miles offshore on their way to Poole Harbour or Studland Bay. The coast is much built up and the beaches of the seaside resorts of Boscombe and Bournemouth exist primarily for holiday makers who want to bathe. If passing close to the beach, six yellow buoys appear at intervals along the shore about a third of a mile out, approximately on the 5 or 10m contour. As tourist-related officials are at pains to point out, these mark surface water drains and not sewers, but they also give mariners a ready guide to position and distance off. The bottom of Poole Bay moves much like the dunes of a desert, so the drain pipes may or may not be exposed above the sea bed at any particular moment.

Boscombe and Bournemouth Piers are major features of the bay. Off Boscombe Pier there is one of a collection of Valentine tanks which have been found on the seabed in Poole Bay. These tanks, fitted with canvas flotation collars and propellers, were developed during the war for amphibious use, evidently with the occasional difficulty. Several sank holding live ammunition.

Boscombe Pier (Plate 10) has structural problems and its head, which includes the old landing place, is closed to the public. As it would cost a fortune either to rebuild or to demolish the pier, this situation is not likely to change. On the other hand Bournemouth Pier (Plate 11) has landing places with at least two metres depth which are available to yachtsmen in an emergency.

Plate 10. The disused Boscombe Pier.

Plate 11. Bournemouth Pier.

Plate 12. Looking north-east at a yacht in the East Looe passage. Notice the wave above the launch breaking on Hook Sands.

In summer a fleet of licensed tripper boats operates from the three levels of landing on either side. Red flags at the seaward end of the pier, flying on either an east or west halyard, denote the side to avoid. Two red flags mean all landing prohibited. On the approach one should watch out for fishing lines emanating from numerous rods on the lower walkways. There is an 8 knot speed restriction to the north of the line between the piers, marked by bright yellow buoys of about 0.6m diameter. The area is patrolled by three fast Narwhal RIBS, of either 3m or 4.5m length.

At weekends yachts seem to find a congenial anchorage to the south-east of Bournemouth Pier. To the west of the pier there are two shallow patches in part composed of fossilised trees, called Durley and Bournemouth Rocks. They are popular fishing and diving spots, but also could constitute a hazard to deeper-draughted vessels in severe weather, should any imprudent skipper choose to be so close in. A mile further out, similar rock patches exist, known as Poole Rocks which are also clumps of fossilised trees jutting up through the sand, and are popular with fishermen and divers.

When entering Poole there are two options: the Swash Channel which is wide, deep and clearly marked, or the East Looe Channel (Plate 12), which is not so easy but can bring a great saving in time and distance for shallow-draughted vessels. When the old groynes along the East Looe Channel shore were removed the channel silted up leaving a minimum depth of barely 1.5m. In 1996 four new rock groynes will be constructed and the existing Midway Path rock groyne will be extended. The groynes will be lit, and it is planned to maintain the channel with a minimum depth of 2m and a minimum width of 50m. When approaching the channel from the east, care should be taken to avoid the shore which is very shallow off the long low crescent-shaped Sandbanks Pavilion. One should only head for the East Looe Buoy when it bears north-west. On passing the buoy, course should be altered to the west to bring the black and yellow post to port, even though this may look at first to be improbably close to the shore. Breaking seas make the presence of Hook Sands obvious if there is any swell, and divers say that there is a dangerous wreck in shallow water at the northern end.

Entering Poole Harbour by the Swash Channel used to be easier by day than by night as few of the channel buoys were lit. However, the new buoyage scheme introduced in 1989 makes things much easier. When large vessels are using the 150m wide deep-water channel, small craft may be more comfortable in the recreational boat channel just to the west of the main channel. Yachts can ignore Poole Fairway Buoy, and will be wise to keep clear of it if happening to be there when it is in use as a turning mark for some major ocean yacht or power boat race. However No 1 Bar Buoy should be rounded to be sure of avoiding the southern extremity of Hook Sands. The historic wreck, marked by a yellow buoy a quarter of a mile to the east of No 3 bar buoy, is dated around 1475. She was a small merchant vessel of about 30m built in the Mediterranean at the time when clinker construction had just given way to carvel, and was carrying finely decorated Spanish pottery. The wreck was found in 1984 after a shift in the sand uncovered enough of the hull to foul a fishing net, and has since been skilfully excavated by the Hamworthy Sub-Aqua Club.

A training bank has been built on the west side of the Swash Channel. Though started in 1876, construction went rather slowly at first and it was only completed in 1927. The stone came by barge from Seacombe Quarry. As intended, the presence of the training bank did markedly increase the scouring effect in the channel to bring it to something around four metres, but recent additional dredging now gives the channel a minimum of six metres. The five large posts marking the training bank are conspicuous, so few should fail to appreciate their significance.

When entering Poole Harbour against the tide at busy times, it may not be wise to cross from the right hand side of the channel

Plate 13. Shell Bay, the Swash Channel and, in the background, Hook Sands can be identified by the paler colour of the water.

Plate 14. There is often plenty of traffic in Poole Harbour entrance. The new ferry can be seen on the right and Blood Alley Lake to the left of Brownsea Island.

to the slacker tide of Shell Bay owing to traffic. There is no such difficulty when leaving, and smaller craft often go inside the main channel buoys to be clear of larger vessels. Shell Bay (Plate 13) is a popular sandy beach with dunes behind, and has four yellow can-shaped buoys laid roughly along the two metre contour marking a 6 knot inshore speed limit to protect bathers.

The Haven Hotel is one of the principal features of the north side of Poole Harbour entrance. A room in this building was used by Marconi between 1898 and 1926 for his most important experiments with early radio and telephones, including the first radio transmission across the Atlantic. He was a sailor, and he owned a yacht called *Electra* which he kept in Poole. The marine radio beacon which used to be on the hotel roof has been removed with the advent of more modern methods of navigation.

One needs to be alert in the narrow entrance of Poole Harbour, as the hazards created by the concentration of traffic and rushing tide are compounded by the existence of the Sandbanks Chain Ferry (Plate 14). A new and larger ferry with an overall length of 74.4m was introduced on 26 January 1994. The ferry captain keeps dual watch on VHF Channels 16 and 14, and, by day, a black ball and flashing white lights at the bow denotes in which direction the ferry is heading. The ferry does not have right of way over other vessels, but craft are well advised to keep clear as serious damage may occur if one is caught by the tide and swept onto the ferry or its chains. Indeed, when at rest on its chains, the ferry has been quite frequently asked to stop by confused small craft sailors. In fog the ferry sounds one long and two short blasts every two minutes, and rings a bell for five seconds every minute if it ever stops in mid-channel.

The chart shows a 3.5m shallow patch 250m west of the Haven Hotel. This is called Chapman's Peak and is of immediate concern to shipping. Yachts leaving the harbour with a strong ebb tide and the intention of keeping to starboard in the channel are often surprised by incoming vessels which turn to port off the Haven Hotel, apparently towards the wrong side of the channel. Ships have to take this diagonal course to avoid Chapman's Peak, and outgoing vessels need to make due allowance by hugging the starboard side of the channel. The spring tidal rate in the entrance is 4.5 knots on the ebb and 3.5 knots on the flood.

Chapter 3

Poole Harbour

The town of Poole has had several economic ups and downs since it was a popular Celtic settlement around the 1st Century BC. The Celts did well from Poole clay pottery, some of which has been unearthed as far away as Hadrian's Wall. To begin with the fortified town of Wareham was the sea port for the area as a subsidiary of the port at Hengistbury Head. As silting occurred, Poole took over and some imposing buildings exist as a reminder of fortunes made when times have been good. In the Late Iron Age and Roman times the south side of Poole Harbour was probably the principal trading centre, rather than the north side as at present. Moreover, the heathland to the south of the harbour was a prosperous farming area.

During World War II Poole became the centre for developing amphibious landing craft and the Royal Marines still have a base at Lake. Nowadays Poole is a busy and prosperous port, a major location for leisure craft and an important source of oil from the Wytch Farm oil field. Although this is the largest onshore oil field in Western Europe, oil-related activities are becoming less obtrusive and the only site left where major oil drilling activity still takes place is on the Goathorn peninsula. Oil from the Poole area is a light crude of good quality, and the field has a life expectancy of a further 20 years.

If entering Poole Harbour is helped by a little local knowledge, so also is finding launching sites for boats on trailers. Sites can be either expensive, restricted or remote. Amongst the best is that at Baiter (Plate 15) a mile to the east of Poole Quay, now that it has been rebuilt to cope with any state of the tide. This is a public

Plate 15. Baiter Slipway. The posts on the right mark the outer end.

Plate 16. The Barfleur *is one of the larger vessels using Poole Harbour.*

slipway where launching, car and trailer parking are all covered by the same modest sum - £5 at the time of writing. The slipway has a gentle gradient, so wading and muscle power may be necessary to launch and recover craft. In spite of this the slip is very popular.

In addition to the 6 knot speed limit applying to the 'quiet areas' such as south and west of Brownsea Island, a summertime speed limit of 10 knots throughout the harbour has been in force for power driven craft in the main channels since April 1994. These limits are firmly enforced, and over thirty prosecutions were made in 1995. One also needs to be wary of obstructing commercial shipping in the main channels. Amongst the larger users is the Truck Line ferry *Barfleur* which uses Poole Harbour almost every day of the year (Plate 16). She is 157m in length, has a draught of 5.2m and is of 20,000 gross tons. Exact indication of shipping movements may be gleaned from listening to the harbour working frequency on VHF Channel 14. Most helpfully, one may also use this channel to ask the depth at the tide gauges at the North Haven Beacon, near the harbour entrance, and at the Ro-Ro Terminal, near the Town Quay. Visual tide gauge boards are also provided at these locations.

Viewed from above, the main channels of Poole take the shape of a tulip. The deeper channels on the north side of Brownsea Island are the functional ones providing through routes, moorings and marinas, whilst the southerly ones provide what many regard as a heavenly cruising ground. All the channels are well marked and there are even signposts at the junctions of channels. As there is abundant information regarding the deep water parts of Poole Harbour, this chapter is confined to areas away from the main channels which are particularly worth visiting. These provide much lovely unspoilt scenery for those with time, patience and a suitably shallow-draughted craft. In addition to the chart, the channels in the shallow parts of the harbour are accurately shown on the Purbeck Ordnance Survey 1:25,000 map. All the islands are privately owned, including, of course, Brownsea Island which is owned by the National Trust, and one has no right of access to any of them above mean high water level - or above the low water level in the case of Brownsea Island.

When bound from the entrance for the southerly part of the harbour, both No 18A and 18 buoys should be left to port to

Plate 17. Redhorn Quay.

avoid Stone Island - or Stony Island as it is called locally - and the gravel and shingle banks to the south. Once past No 18 buoy, one will be left choosing between Blood Alley Lake, or South Deep. Blood Alley Lake is shallow but makes a good spot to anchor if one can get in, especially when looking for shelter from a north wind. There is a little more depth of water at Whiteground Lake, just to the north-west of Furzey Island pier. Blood Alley, incidentally, owes its name to a confrontation between the Revenue and the Men of Poole, who were a pretty villainous smuggling lot.

Plate 18. Brands Bay looking north-east. South of the moorings the channel is unmarked, narrow and shallow.

As a venturesome alternative to South Deep, Redhorn Lake offers tranquillity and charm. The deep but narrow channel is marked with starboard hand posts, but they are not quite in the channel itself and in some cases need to be kept at a distance of 30m or so. The deepest pools for anchoring are just north of Redhorn Quay (Plate 17), where one can land on the gravel spit and, though 2m or more can be found, there is not much room, especially taking into account the moorings which are in the centre of the channel (Plate 18). Further into Brands Bay the creeks are very pretty and full of wildlife, but too shallow to be suitable for anything other than rowing dinghies (Plate 19). The

Plate 19. Brands Bay near Mead Point.

channel divides at Mead Point where there is a bird watchers' hide and a hard landing on the western side. Brands Bay is part of the Studland Heath National Nature Reserve leased by the Nature Conservation Council from the National Trust. The name may have been derived from Henry Brand, born 1525. It is said that in Tudor times the bay was notorious as a centre of piracy and smuggling.

The channel at South Deep has a shoal in the middle and mud spits have been known to form at the edges. In the past, the posts were moved to comply with natural channel evolution, but now larger permanent lit beacons have been installed, particularly with the ferry service to Furzey Island in mind. There are two ferries which service the oil production rig on Furzey Island, the 36m *Furzey Squirrel* - an allusion to the now rarely-found red variety living there - and the 13m crew boat *Sherwood,* named after the major Wytch Farm oil reservoir. To avoid a rude awakening, care should be taken to avoid obstructing them by anchoring in the fairway. There is a notice on one of the posts to this effect. Furzey, by the way, was an alternative name for gorse.

Goathorn (Plate 20) used to be an embarkation point for clay brought by rail from Norden and the Newton Clay Works between 1905 and 1937. It is a much loved anchorage, but can be uncomfortable in certain combinations of wind and current, when the reach off the west side of Goathorn may be preferred. There are cables marked by shore beacons running between Furzey Island and Goathorn which often used to foul anchors in the past. Now that these cables have been buried they are less of a problem, but still have to be considered.

At one time there was a plan to build an island on Hook Sands in order to exploit the part of the Sherwood oil field under Poole Bay. Happily the plan was abandoned, and the oil field has been reached by drilling sideways from Goathorn, the distance of 7.8km verging on a world record. The Deutag T47 Rig is 60m high and requires considerably more power than the other Wych Farm sites. It is likely to complete the task towards the end of 1996.

Newton Bay (Plate 21) to the south is exceptionally pretty and worth a visit in a small and flat-bottomed boat, but it will be a job to find anything that can be called a channel. Central marshes divide the bay into east and west areas. The western side has

Plate 20. Yachts off Goathorn with Furzey Island behind.

Plate 21. Newton Bay looking north-east.

Plate 22. Looking south-west from Newton Bay's east shore.

enough water for small craft to moor just south of Cleaval Point, and the eastern shore has some sandy beaches suitable for landing on by dinghy at high water (Plate 22). At low water there is only mud. Once ashore on the eastern bank there is woodland and thick undergrowth, tortoiseshell butterflies, and peace

Plate 23. Ower Bay looking north-east.

Plate 24. One of the sparse channel markers in Ower Bay.

except, perhaps, for the occasional clank from the oil rig. The name Newton, by the way, is derived from Edward I's proposal to build a new pottery town there in 1286 in an attempt to revive the prosperity of the south harbour. Evidently it never happened.

Ower Bay (Plate 23) is much silted up like Newton. In comparatively recent times a sailing ferry used to work between Hamworthy, Wareham and a landing stage on the south side of the bay called Ower Passage. There are traces of the landing stage supports still left, opposite an old windlass, and some withies, though not enough of them to indicate clearly the meagre channels (Plate 24). Ower is the Saxon name for 'shore'. In the Middle Ages Ower was the major port of Purbeck, where the stone, including the so-called Purbeck 'marble', was exported. It remained so until the Great Fire of London in 1666 when, presumably, Ower was found to be unsuitable for the increased need. From then on Swanage became the principal port for building stone.

Ower Passage House on the shore line was an alehouse when the port was still active and has a smugglers cache. The occupier receives a pound of pepper each year from the Ancient Order of Purbeck Marblers and Stonecutters, the medieval trade guild which still regulates the stone industry.

Deep-keel yachts can seldom get beyond the Old Roman Causeway between Green, once Helen's, Island and Cleaval Point as the channel becomes narrow and shallow, but shoal-draughted craft will be able to continue the circuit round the

Plate 25. Looking north-east towards Shipstal Point on the left and Long Island on the right.

Plate 26. Looking north-west at Shipstal Point.

Plate 27. Looking north from over Wych Farm. Middlebere Lake is on the left and Wych Lake on the right.

'stamen' of the Poole Harbour 'tulip' via Ramshorn Lake where, to the west, an array of round coloured floats marking shellfish beds will be seen. At the north end of Ramshorn Lake one can choose whether to return to the busy world of the north part of the harbour, or take the Upper Wych Channel to another attractive cruising area. The words Wych and Wytch, by the way, are derived from the Saxon name for the Corfe River which was the Wichen. In turn Wichen may have derived from the word 'wics' meaning dairy farm, a reflection upon the time when the heathland south of the harbour was still wooded and fertile.

The Upper Wych Channel leads to an anchorage off Shipstal Point (Plate 25), more sheltered from the west than Goathorn. One can take a dinghy to the beach (Plate 26), and then walk through a bird sanctuary to the village of Arne or take a flat-bottomed dinghy, such as an inflatable, up the wild and secluded marshes of Middlebere or Wych Lake (Plate 27). Few channel markers exist after Round Island, and such vestigial channels as can be found lie elusively in wide stretches of mudflat between the saltmarsh beds. The channels have become much silted up during the past 40 years. For example, old Imray charts show a

Plate 28. Looking south-west down Middlebere Lake.

Plate 29. Looking north-west over Arne Bay.

minimum of one metre at chart datum in the channel leading to Middlebere Quay, where clay used to be loaded. This came from Norden by a tramway built in 1806, reputed to be the first ever made in Dorset. Nowadays one might find a metre of water at high water springs in the channel at best. Exploration requires persistence and patience, but will be rewarded by a variety of bird life and splendid isolation.

If attempting to enter Middlebere Lake, initially the channel will be found close to the marsh on the south side. Thereafter the channel is more in the middle. There is an ancient central post at the first bend with traces of red paint on it, suggesting that it should once have been left to port, but the channel may well have moved since it was put in position. The channel soon narrows after the first bend - if one has been lucky enough to find it in the first place. Middlebere is mainly wooded on the north side and white egrets, sandwich terns and warblers in the reed beds can be seen against a background of dark heathland colours and the distant Purbeck Hills (Plate 28).

Wych Lake is much the same as Middlebere. If anything, the channel is more tortuous and difficult to find. The only structures to be seen are pylons where power cables cross the Corfe River, at a point where there used to be a ferry. Hidden in a Wych Heath Corsican pine wood plantation, however, is the 20 acre gathering station for the ten well sites in the area where the oil is processed to separate it from gas and water residues. From here the oil is pumped through an 0.46m pipe 90km to the BP Marine Terminal at the Hamble.

One has to make a brief return to civilisation to get to the Wareham Channel from Shipstal Point. Initially it is necessary to give a wide berth to the shallow Arne Bay (Plate 29), and follow the channel back to Balls Lake. Though both Balls Lake and Wills Cut are marked like channels, in fact they are only deeper than their surroundings owing to the scouring effect of passing vessels, so it could be necessary to go a long way eastward to reach the deep water passage. Once in the Wareham Channel, one heads westward following the large channel marks past Hamworthy's industrial scenery. In the long Wareham Channel reach there is time to enjoy the view over Arne Heath to the Purbeck Hills, though concentration may be necessary at the licence-holders' water skiing site between buoys 73 and 82. As

Plate 30. Looking east over the River Frome. Wareham Bridge can be seen at the bottom left.

Plate 31. Wareham Quay.

the channel narrows and does its first turn to the left, one is guided by an abundance of channel markers except, perhaps, in early spring when several may have been carried away by ice coming down the river. Meanders of the Frome River double the direct distance to South Bridge at Wareham so, with the 4 knot speed limit, the passage up river will take nearly an hour. The narrow channel lies between walls of reeds giving little room between passers-by and the chain of about 500 moored craft along the left hand bank (Plate 30).

The chart indicates salmon holes where they congregate and are occasionally netted for research. Anchoring is prohibited here, but in practice there is too much river traffic to anchor anywhere without blocking the fairway. The trip up the river is an enjoyable experience. Changes of scene come at Ridge Wharf, where one can get a berth though it is advisable to ring beforehand (01929) 552650, and Redcliffe, where there is a launching slip. Ridge Wharf used to be the terminal of another railway for transporting clay, this time from Furzebrooke. Tidal range at Ridge Wharf is about two metres, and boats with draughts of 1.5m can usually get as far as Redcliffe, after which the river gets noticeably shallower. As a general guide a draught of 1.2m is the limit for Wareham, but in favourable tidal circumstances vessels of two metres have been known to get there.

Wareham stands within the rectangle of its own low earth ramparts which, in excavations since the Second World War, have been shown to originate from the 9th Century. Wareham was chosen by King Alfred as a major base when fighting the Danes, and the grid street pattern is probably of Saxon origin. There are many fine buildings in Wareham, especially of the later 18th Century, and there is a statue of Lawrence of Arabia in the church, carved by his friend Eric Kennington.

Most skippers will be quite happy to go alongside at the charming Wareham Quay (Plate 31) and savour the delights of the town, but craft which can get under the bridge are permitted to go up to the tidal limit of the river. Anyone wishing to go further will have to seek consent from the owner of the adjacent land. The normal tidal limit (NTL) of the Frome is shown on the 1:25000 ordnance survey map about a mile above South Bridge. Propellers are likely to be overwhelmed with ranunculus weed in summer, and fishermen should be respected. On the other hand,

Plate 32. The lower reaches of the Piddle River.

the river is deep and has a specially attractive southern view over fields and woodland with the Purbecks beyond. Wildlife is abundant and one would be unlucky not to see at least one kingfisher.

The Piddle, Puddle, North or Trent river is as attractive on a smaller scale as the South or Frome river. For the most part the Piddle is narrow and deep (Plate 32), but a tricky shallow threshold limits navigation by anything other than dinghies or canoes. A new bridge has been built two kilometres up the river opposite Sandford Farm. Visitors are rare and this means that wildlife such as moorhens, yellow wagtails, kingfishers and reed warblers abound. Even on a Sunday it is quite possible to encounter more herons than people.

To get to the Piddle, one has to turn north-west from the Frome when approximately quarter of a mile ENE of Swineham Point, whereupon one will almost certainly have difficulty in finding the channel. The first 250m is shallow and is best undertaken with oars, but from the punt moorings onwards the channel has two metres depth up to the new bridge. As one heads up the river past reed and grassy banks, the water becomes fresher and clearer revealing a sandy bottom and some lively trout. Eventually one comes upon an industrial estate and power lines to the right before Wareham North Bridge with its somewhat less appealing odours. There is not much to be said for these, but the lower reaches are remarkably peaceful and attractive, best visited in spring or autumn to avoid prolific weed. The statutory tidal limit is at North Bridge, but even if one did have permission to proceed beyond this point, portage would be necessary.

Chapter 4

Studland, Swanage & Durlston Bays

S tudland Bay is a popular yacht anchorage, well sheltered from the prevailing wind, and the chalk promontories on the north side of Handfast Point add much to the attractiveness of this beautiful bay (Plate 33). The Old Harry Ledges should be treated with respect when entering from the south, especially in an easterly or south-easterly on an ebb tide. There is an apt local saying 'If the wind is in the east, Old Harry's Ledge can be a beast'. When entering from Poole Harbour one should not forget the good honest Purbeck stone of the training wall. Dinghies under oars may be able to slip over it around high water near Pilot Point, at the south end of Shell Bay, but it is inadvisable to try to cross it in any other circumstances. The wall is more deeply covered at the southern end, finishing a little beyond the most seaward red beacon. A red lit buoy has replaced the wooden structure off the southern end of the training bank.

The bay is generally shallow at the north end, and very shallow over Milkmaid Bank, so decp-keeled yachts tend to keep to the

Plate 33. Studland Bay looking south-east towards Handfast Point. A power boat has just gone through the race off Old Harry.

Plate 34. The corner of Studland Bay.

south of a line between the training wall outer beacon structure and Knoll Slip. This slip has now been moved 300m south of the National Trust buildings, where there is an assortment of parked craft such as Hobie Cats, windsurfers, ski boats and hire canoes. For a small charge visiting boats on trailers can be launched here over the double bank of reinforced concrete railway sleepers, though jet skis are not allowed.

The beach was the scene of wartime invasion practice landings which were witnessed by Winston Churchill, in company with Generals Montgomery and Eisenhower, from the impressive Fort Henry Bunker within the grounds of the Manor House Hotel at the attractive Redend Point. There is another building behind the bunker open to seaward which was a gun emplacement, and an

Plate 35. The beach at Studland.

unusually solid-looking circular pill box on a square base on the beach below. Nowadays Studland Bay (Plate 34) is popular with swimmers in summer and walkers the rest of the time. There is also a naturists' beach opposite Milkmaid Bank. Bathers are protected from high speed craft by a line of some eight yellow 5 knot speed limit buoys. Apart from the two northerly buoys and the most southerly one, these are in at least three metres of water. At the south end of the bay one can land and anchor anywhere (Plate 35), though one should avoid some offshore rocks around Redend Point. South east of Redend Point there is a patch of rocks called the Seven Sisters and, further out, Blind Rock, both marked with posts topped by a round mooring buoy. Three of the Sisters appear at a good low tide but it has to be an exceptional tide for all seven to appear. Blind Rock is now called Simon's Rock by some in memory of a lad who died of cancer.

The first bay on turning east towards Handfast Point is called Road Cove. It seems that carts used to be taken to the base of the cliff at low tide to collect fresh water from the spring under Warren Wood. The next bay 0.3 nm to the west of the point is called Pilot's Path. It was here that the Poole Harbour sailing pilot vessels often used to lie awaiting business, and a path called Pilot's Path led up the cliff to Handfast Point from where incoming vessels were spotted. There is still evidence of this severely steep path towards the east end of the cliffs. If one succeeds in the ascent, the continuation from the cliff top is identifiable, but much overgrown with brambles. To the east of Pilot's Path there are two bays without names, followed by Wood Cove below Studland Wood. The beaches between the folds of the easternmost cliffs of the mainland, the promontories called the Yards, make reasonable landings, but it is only possible to get from one to another at low tide.

Studland is exposed to the east but is well sheltered from the prevailing wind. One can anchor anywhere in Studland Bay, with something to be said for going as far in as prudence will allow, short of fishermen's moorings in shallow water near Blind Rock. Modern charts do not show foul ground off the Yards as they used to, but fishermen say that they still use 56lb coal merchants' weights there instead of anchors, to avoid catching wreck debris on the bottom. This came about as a result of magnetic mines being dropped in Poole harbour entrance during the war. As in the entrances of many other ports before the secret of the

Plate 36. Handfast Point. Little Pinnacle Rock and The Pinnacle can be seen in the background. Note the reef off Old Harry.

magnetic mine was discovered, many ships were sunk in the Swash Channel and the wrecks were dragged to the Yards where they remained until the war was over. There are some more Valentine tanks hereabouts on the seabed too.

On calm days exploration of the rocks off Handfast Point (Plate 36) can make an enjoyable dinghy or canoe outing though, as on many parts of this coast, there is a rather over-plentiful growth of Japanese seaweed to contend with in summer. One can best land on the north side of the separate island called No Man's Land at a spot opposite a window in the white wall of chalk, where there is sand rather than rocks, in the approach. This is supposedly the site of 'Studland Castle' shown on a 16th Century map. It may not have been more than a wartime gun emplacement, and there appears to be no sign of it now, as might be expected if it was built on chalk foundations.

Old Harry, a medieval name for Satan himself, has not changed much in 100 years, though he is getting gradually thinner. His wife used to be a slightly diminutive and portly companion, but she became much dwarfed in the severe storm of 1896.

At high water one can now take a dinghy between Handfast

Point and No Man's Land, where old photographs show a ridge nearly as high as the cliff. An archway will be seen at the west end of No Man's Land, which has another at right angles, visible from the other side, penetrating the southern tip. When going round Old Harry to seaward one needs to keep outside the reefs to the east and south. In clear weather local fishermen line up the white-painted tourist information centre at Swanage, which is actually called the White House, with Ballard Point on a bearing of 222°Mag. This line clears the Old Harry Ledges with a minimum depth of 2.5m, as well as all the underwater hazards down to Ballard Point.

In the bay to the south of Old Harry one will find some deeper water and virtually no tidal stream. Another arch runs through the first headland south of No Man's Land, and there are narrow grey beaches within the coves to the south. Pebbles from these beaches used to be collected for facing local houses, but there is little else to do except, perhaps, to contemplate the consequences of a cliff fall. The first stack south of Handfast Point, called Little Pinnacle on the chart, is better known locally as either the Haystack, Turf Rickrock or the Wedge, depending upon where you come from. There is a good sized green-roofed cave just to its west, sometimes thought to be Parson's Barn, but there is no doubt that the magnificent authentic Parson's Barn, used by smugglers and deriving its name from some wry allusion to bygone parsons' affluence, collapsed in 1963. As it has maintained its pointed shape, there is no argument over Pinnacle Rock; however it must have lost some height as old photographs show it as high as the cliff and with a small crown of grass on the peak. At the turn of the 19th Century, peregrine falcons nested in a hole at the top, but they would certainly not have remained there during the Second World War as the Pinnacle was beside four old tanks on the cliff top which were used by aircraft as a target for live ammunition firing. There was another target on the sea, and the whole area was showered with 20mm cannon cartridges from Spitfires and Hurricanes. Divers and fishermen still find corroded shell case ends under the cliffs, and hundreds have been gathered on the Handfast peninsula.

Two hundred metres south, between the Pinnacle and Ballard Point, there is another deep cave with a rocky threshold, and towards Ballard Point there is, at a geological fault, a circular pattern in the cliff face used by the locals to place a large drying

Plate 37. Ballard Point in the foreground with a submerged ledge showing off it. Another dark smudge showing in the water half way down the cliff is Argyll Rock.

rock about 50m off the cliff. This is like a giant table top, and is called Argyll Rock after one of several unfortunate fishing vessels which have encountered it (Plate 37). When rounding Ballard Point, where another large cave will be seen, it can be advisable to keep 100m offshore to avoid a ledge and the turbulence which develops where the Swanage Bay eddy, known as The Outset, meets the south-going main Poole Bay stream.

Swanage is a small and pleasant seaside resort and, as one would expect, it is sheltered from the prevailing wind, but wide open to the east. No doubt it was an easterly that drove 120 ships of a Danish invasion reinforcement fleet ashore at Peveril in the year 877 AD, much to the relief of King Alfred and his subjects who were thought, according to some records, to be shadowing the Danes in a rather smaller fleet. The following year King Alfred achieved his great victory over the Danes at Edington.

The tidal currents are interesting (Appendix II), and those who wish to study the movement of the surface water for themselves will benefit from observing how the Mowlem Stream, otherwise known as The Brook, flows across the bay. Being a culvert for Swanage quarries, this turns a distinctive yellow after heavy rainfall. John Mowlem, after whom the stream was named, was a Swanage boy who went to London, there to build a most successful business in the stone trade. Eventually he returned home to Swanage and became a great local benefactor.

When the wind is from the north, the bay offers an attractive alternative anchorage to Studland, and is also a useful holding point when waiting for a favourable Channel tide. It is not built up at the north end, and one can anchor at the turn in the bay where Ballard Cliff comes to an end. Deep water, good holding ground on sand or shingle and good shelter from north-west to north-east winds will be found at this anchorage known as Pundfield. It seems this may have been the Pondfield where the owner of Whitecliff kept swans, and the spot where King John's crown jewels and accoutrements were landed when he made the keep of Corfe Castle the state treasury. Corfe Castle has other claims to fame. In the Civil War the royalist garrison under Lady Bankes held out against siege for some years and only succumbed in 1645 when a defender betrayed them. Afterwards it was ordered that the castle be destroyed, but despite all the explosives used by the military engineers much of it still stands, a great tribute to its Norman origins.

There are six byelaw buoys running the length of Swanage Beach, approximately 400m offshore, restricting speed to 5 knots. The most northerly buoy is in six metres of water, the depth reducing gradually to three metres at the south buoy. They give a useful pilotage line to clear the dangerous Tanville Ledges off the large red-bricked Grand Hotel, and the smaller Phippard's Ledge, off an apartment block with a flat roof. Incidentally Evans Rock, way out in the bay off Shippard's Ledge, is said to be a heap of quarried rocks which must have either been jettisoned there at some time or have gone down with a stone barge.

There is no harbour authority at Swanage (Plate 38). The moorings are all privately owned; but visitors can always make arrangements for using a mooring by applying to the pleasure boat operators at the stone quay, the lifeboat house, or the angling club next door. Moorings vary considerably in capacity: for example one should, in particular, avoid picking up one of the three small white buoys which are there to mark the seagoing limits for hire boats. Beach byelaws ban all boats and motorized inflatables from landing on the beach, but most mariners will find it more convenient anyway to use the free Parish Slipway or the

Plate 38. Swanage Harbour looking south-east.

Plate 39. The ebb tide race off Peveril Point.

Stone Pier. Incidentally anyone hankering to visit Corfe Castle by steam locomotive, when perhaps galebound, will be delighted to find that the Swanage Railway will oblige for a modest sum. Swanage station is in the centre of the town. Turn right along the shore towards the town from the slipway; on arrival at the Mowlem Institute look for Station Road on the other side of Institute Road.

The derelict wooden jetty inshore of the pier is called the First Pier, built in 1859 for the export of Purbeck stone. This was the time when Swanage was the key point for a huge stone industry which provided, for example, the stone used in the construction of both Salisbury Cathedral and Westminster Abbey besides countless other works. Going east from the pier one will see new waterside properties by the Wellington clock tower, but a marina proposal was opposed by local opinion, and was finally brought to a halt in the House of Lords in 1988.

Close into the shore by the lifeboat slip there is a line of rocks running parallel to the Peveril Ledges. This has a high point called The Berry which, though marked with a post, still manages to discommode unwary visitors. The Berry does serve to provide some protection to the lifeboat slip from the west. There is a launching slip for trailer-borne craft between two small piers by the lifeboat house, towards Peveril Point.

Peveril Point itself has twin arms with a rock between them, visible at low water. These arms extend well to seaward in the form of parallel vertical underwater walls of broken shell limestone, which kick up dangerously steep waves when the tide is running. The race that develops there on a spring ebb tide is particularly wicked in a strong south-easterly wind, and not much less so in a strong south-westerly wind (Plate 39). Though the race extends well out into the bay in a south-easterly direction from Peveril Point, the worst of it occurs between the unlit red can buoy off the point and the shore, leading to the obvious prescript that one may avoid trouble by going outside the buoy. Nevertheless locals going between Durlston Head and Swanage will cut the corner by half when conditions allow. Of course they know when the tides are weak, and also know that there is a minimum of two metres of water to seaward of a sewer outlet box where gulls gather. Those who choose to follow their example should watch out for numerous lobster pot floats which will be submerged when the tide is running. It should be mentioned that the old coastguard station overlooks the ledge, and is now manned in summer by the National Coastwatch Institution when the tide is ebbing, and at weekends. Coverage will extend into winter as more volunteers can be found. NCI have even installed a radar and claim a number of helpful 'sightings'.

Durlston Bay, to the south of Peveril, looks rather inhospitable from seaward, and though one can get shelter there in a south-westerly, the seabed has, in addition to the sandy bottom, areas of kelp-covered rocks on which anchors easily get fouled. Do not anchor close to a round yellow buoy at 12m depth in the middle of the bay as this marks the Durlstone Country Park hydrophone mounted on a seabed tripod. A steep path will be found up the cliff to Durlston Castle at the south end of the bay and others at the Peveril Point end; but landing on the rocky shore is not easy, especially at low tide. The bay is good for lobsters, and there is little stream inshore. Durlston Castle was built in 1864 for the benefit of the public by George Burt, John Mowlem's nephew, partner and eventual heir.

The rocks at the base of Durlston Head (Plate 40) can be approached quite closely. On the ebb a tide race will be found right up to the cliff resulting in big breaking seas in a south-westerly gale. Curiously, there is said to be a natural gas outlet some 200m south of the stone globe on the cliff.

Durlston Head is the start of the picturesque cliffs which run all the way to St Aldhelm's (or Alban's) Head. One can generally find deep water close to the cliffs as shown on the chart, but one should respect perpendicular Purbeck limestone, famous for its durability, when there is an onshore breeze.

Durlston Country Park is situated above Durlston Head where interesting wildlife projects run by Rolf Williams are open to the public. There is a cliff camera sited just east of Tilly Whim (Plate 41), which can be traversed and zoomed to monitor any object in sight at sea or on land from the park centre. The camera is mainly used for watching a guillemot colony during the breeding season. This is the most easterly colony on the south coast and boat skippers are asked not to disturb the birds by going close to the cliffs at this point. The live transmissions of the hydrophone can also be heard at the country club. Bottle-nosed dolphins are commonly heard on the hydrophone rather than common dolphins which tend to stay well offshore. Rolf Williams welcomes reports of whale, dolphin and shark sightings

Plate 40. Durlston Head looking north.

Plate 41. Anvil Point. The Tilly Whim landing is adjacent to the valley on the right of the lighthouse. The Ragged Rocks are at the base of the cliffs to the left of the lighthouse.

anywhere along the coast, and in particular the less common varieties such as the harbour porpoise, the striped dolphin and Risso's dolphin with the date and time, the species and number. He, or his answerphone, can be found on (01929) 421111.

Plate 42. Looking south over Durlston Point and Anvil Point. The flat water inshore indicates the east-going eddy. Refer to the tidal stream atlases at the back for details.

Plate 43. The Tilly Whim landing, caves and the measured distance beacons.

Chapter 5

Anvil Point To St Aldhelm's Head

Anvil Point's principal feature is the lighthouse built of local stone and opened in 1881 by Neville Chamberlain's prominent and powerful father, Joseph, when he was President of the Board of Trade. Its powerful light with a range of 24 miles flashes every ten seconds. The inshore tidal stream up to about half a mile off Anvil Point often runs in the opposite direction to the main offshore ebb, a point well worth noting when looking for tidal assistance or calmer water (Plate 42).

A pair of measured distance beacons will be seen just to the east of Anvil Point and in line with them are the Tilly Whim caves. George Tilly was a quarry owner and a whim was a gantry crane which, incidentally, proved to be just as useful for lifting contraband as lowering prime building stone. To the west of the caves there is an old landing place called the Tilly Whim Landing, or Tilly Whim Steps, after the large rough-hewn steps above, which can look from seaward like a well-constructed quay (Plate 43). It is one of several loading points for stone boats along this coast, known as the 'Back of the Cliff', all of which must have required great skill to use with unhandy craft. The Tilly Whim approach is from the south-east along the line of the 'wharf'. It is not a satisfactory place to try to get alongside, even in flat calm, as there is an underwater rock shelf coming out at the most convenient berthing point. Square recesses cut into the rock face look as if they may have taken beams of some sort, possibly to hold craft off this ledge. They would have to be portable, as no permanent structure would survive in such an exposed position. If disembarkation is possible, there is a footpath from the steps to Durlston Country Park after an initial scramble up the cliff face. The Tilly Whim caves are closed as there is considered to be a risk of roof falls.

From Anvil Point for three-quarters of a mile to the west, giant blocks of rock lie along the water line at the base of the rather savagely beautiful cliffs, known as the Ragged Rocks. It was on this shore that the large sailing ship *Alexandranova of Liverpool* went ashore in a violent storm on 28 April 1882 with the loss of all her crew. Divers have found her remains which are now mainly ballast. The quarry at the point she struck is called Topmast, as one of her topmasts was found there, together with one of her 77 crew who perished, presumably doing lookout duty.

Just to the west of the westerly pair of measured distance beacons (Plate 44) there is an eerie cave called Long Hole (Plate 45). This has a depth of six metres at its entrance which allows waterborne exploration. Five hundred metres further along the cliff is a huge gaping recess in the cliff called Blacker's Hole (Plate 46), which comes into view when rounding St Aldhelm's Head from the west. It is another site where peregrine falcons used to breed and now provides a summer residence for jackdaws. If determined to visit Blacker's Hole by sea, one can find a line to the west of the entrance where a strip of sand indicates a path between the rocks. Landing on the dome of rock within is decidedly tricky. Nevertheless the lifeboat has been in to rescue errant rock climbers. It was said in the 19th Century that there was room for three fishing boats alongside in the cave,

Plate 44. The cliffs to the west of Anvil Point and the The Ragged Rocks. Long Hole is just west of the line of the measured distance beacons and Blacker's Quarry can be seen towards the left of the picture.

Plate 45. Long Hole.

but there must have been a roof fall since as it would not be possible now. In extraordinarily calm conditions it would be possible to land on the black potholed ledge below Blacker's Hole quarry to the east. At low water one can get into the hole from here, or one can climb the cliff. Initially there is a precipitous ascent which turns into a steep path.

Plate 46. Blacker's Hole.

Another attractive fair-weather old quarry landing place will be found at Dancing Ledge (Plate 47), so named because the much quarried sea ledge was humorously suggested to be as big and flat as a dance floor. Nine strata of rock were taken, much of it to create Ramsgate's sea and harbour wall. One should not try to land on the sloping seaward face, as this is where waves dance, but go in at the south-west tip, where the ledge has been cut away and there is deep water (Plate 48). This was where the stone barges went alongside. Of course it would be suicidal to try to approach even at this spot with any sea or swell running.

The rutways for the stone-carrying horn carts can be seen leading to the south-west end, besides four recesses for gibbets and a hole on the edge of the rock for securing berthing lines. A swimming pool will also be found, which was made by the quarrymen for Durnford Preparatory School due to the influence of the headmaster, Thomas Pellatt, who owned the land. Dancing Ledge is particularly popular with rock climbers and large numbers are often to be seen on the cliffs. After landing, one can clamber up the rock face above the sea ledge to the upper ledge,

Plate 47. Dancing Ledge from above.

Plate 48. Dancing Ledge veiwed from the east.

and then follow a path to Langton Matravers via Spyway Barn. The promontory just to the east of Dancing Ledge is called Green Point, and the rock off it is called Bower's Rock.

Other quarries are visible along the cliffs to the west of Dancing Ledge such as Hedbury (Plate 49) and Mike's Quarry. All the stone from these quarries used to go out by sea via stone-transporting boats. These were strong, inelegant, flat-bottomed craft of about seven metres length, which were towed around to the site by ketch-rigged sailing barges, and were small enough to get inshore under the gibbets. They were pointed at both ends and were normally rowed by two men with sweeps, but they did also have a lug sail for use when conditions suited. Though they were

Plate 49. Hedbury Quarry.

built very strongly, with oak frames and one inch planks, such craft loaded with about six tons of stone did sink from time to time, whereupon their crews had to cling firmly to their buoyant wooden sweeps.

The 24 superimposed beds of Purbeck limestone lying between Swanage and Chapmans Pool are angled away from the sea. The top layer is Purbeck marble which, because it can be highly polished, has been prized since Roman times. The lowest layer is Purbeck Portland stone and is also prized as it is even-textured, non-shelly, white and good for carving. As the beds incline to the north, the Portland Beds come to the surface along the shore; hence the many coastline quarries. The diminutive Coach House museum at Langton Matravers is an excellent source of interesting information on Purbeck geology and the stone trade.

There is an old mounted cannon pointing seaward at Hedbury Quarry, with two opinions upon its origin. It may have been one of several salvaged *Halsewell* cannons (see next page) brought to Hedbury for some reason; or it may have been part of several batteries established during the French invasion scare of 1803. Hedbury Quarry, by the way, was famous at one time for its stone sinks.

Just past Mike Bower's Quarry, there is a cave which can at times be identified audibly. It is the Pig and Whistle Cave which

Plate 50. Seacombe Quarry looking north.

Plate 51. Seacombe Quarry from sea level. The loading rock is the flat ledge towards the right with the central of the three caves behind it.

grunts like a pig when a wave goes in at a certain state of the tide, then whistles as the wave recedes.

Given, it needs to be said, very calm conditions, the next quarry with sea access is Seacombe (Plate 50). The best place to land, though not for keel boats, is where the barges used to go alongside on the east side of the principal ledge, opposite a large cave. Best spot of all is well up the ledge towards the cave, but care should be taken to avoid a rock sticking out from a deep crevice dividing the ledge (Plate 51). Rings let into the ledge have long gone, but suitable knobs of rock will be found to secure to if one has long enough warps. There used to be two other large caves on the west side called Mike's and Willie's Caves, separated by a circular lump, shaped more or less like a round cake tin, called Watch Rock, but in the winter of 1994 Mike's Cave completely collapsed.

A footpath leads up Seacombe Bottom to the village of Worth Matravers. One can pause to look into the vast subterranean galleries now enjoyed as a shelter by cattle and bats, and also take a cautious glance into the deep and beautiful gorge to the west of the path which was a former quarry too. Whilst it is tempting to explore further, the state of the roof support must be a little questionable.

On 6 January 1786 a harrowing shipwreck took place on the rocks a quarter of a mile west of Seacombe with the loss of the captain, his daughters, and many of the passengers and crew. The vessel was the *Halsewell*, an East Indiaman on passage from

Dover to Bengal. The ship had sprung a serious leak off Berry Head and was returning to Portsmouth when she was overcome by a severe storm from the south. Unable to make to windward she anchored, but in the early hours of the morning she dragged into the cliffs where she rapidly broke up. Some of the crew were able to get from the rigging to a cave in the cliff face, and others scaled a flat sloping face from the sea, now called Halsewell Rock (Plate 52). Only when daylight came did two crewmen manage to climb to the cliff top and raise help, by which time only 82 of the original 240 people on board were still alive.

Divers have found numerous artefacts from the wreck, some of which can be seen in the Dorchester museum. In addition a rather poignantly pretty mirror hangs above the main door in Worth Matravers church. Various other objects are scattered around Dorset, but little was left to salvage from this once proud ship.

The *Halsewell* wreck site is half way between Seacombe and another landing point called Winspit (Plate 53), once Windspit. It lies between two bold hills known as East and West Man, of interest to etymologists as the word 'man' is one of the few, if not the only, Celtic word to survive in local place names. There are extensive coastal quarries on either side of Winspit Bottom which, for example, provided the stone for building Allhallows School. The unmade road from Winspit Bottom leads up to another valley and thence to the village of Worth Matravers. It goes past the house of a one time quarryman and great local character nicknamed Billy Winspit, and is bordered by some well-defined medieval terraced fields called strip-lynchets. West Winspit was the last of the coastal quarries to close down, still being in use until the early 1960s.

Plate 52. The cliff between Seacombe and Winspit looking west. Halsewell Rock is the large sloping rock towards the right.

Plate 53. Winspit Quarry.

The small-craft landing point is opposite the trough of the valley, and requires careful pilotage at the best of times, due to a large rock lying off the two ledges which together form a miniature dock. This flat light-coloured rock is clearly visible in the narrow entrance and should be left to port on entry. Inside there is a metre or two of water, and quite a convenient berthing spot alongside the left hand ledge. It has to be said that one could emulate the *Halsewell* easily enough by trying to land here in anything but absolutely calm conditions.

Plate 54. Crab Hole.

As one progresses towards St Aldhelm's Head a semi-circular recess in the cliffs may be seen 500m to the west of Winspit. This is a rocky little bay called Crab Hole (Plate 54), with no access from above and no easy landing. If one is very close into the shore for some reason, there is a ledge to avoid just to the east of Crab Hole.

St Aldhelm's Head (Plate 55) is, of course, the major and highest coastal feature in the immediate area. The old coastguard lookout station is now manned by the NCI at weekends. It will have been noticed that the title St Aldhelm's Head has been used, rather than the corruption 'St Alban's Head', which came into use many years ago as a result of an ordnance surveyor's difficulty with local pronunciation. There is no doubt that the headland and ledge were named after the St Aldhelm born in 739 AD who did actually visit the headland whilst awaiting favourable winds to take him south on a mission to confer with the Pope. Surely this extraordinarily talented scholar and brilliantly capable Saxon bishop deserves to be remembered by his authentic name.

The plateau below the headland plain on the east side of the point rejoices in the name Ring-Bum Gardens, apparently because this plot used to be cultivated by the coastguards, who managed to grow two crops of potatoes a year. The low-lying most southerly tip is called Buttery Corner, though locals believe this should possibly be Battery Corner.

A diminutive 12th Century chapel dedicated to St Aldhelm stands on the top of the headland, behind the coastguard lookout station. There are various theories for its existence: it may have been a landmark combined with a chantry in the cause of sailors, or one may prefer the melancholy legend that it was erected by the father of a young bride, drowned with her husband when sailing round the point in 1140. The story goes that whilst the father proudly watched the newly-weds at sea from the top of the 108m high headland, a storm got up and their boat capsized.

Perhaps they got caught by the race, which is well known by experienced navigators for its ferocity at spring tides. This is created by a four mile long precipitous underwater ledge, which, by halving the depth, can throw up furious breaking waves on the tidal lee. Even when the surrounding area is flat calm, a boisterous sea develops to be heard at some distance. This can be a chilling sound at night. As might be expected, the race is at its

Plate 55. St Aldhelm's Head, looking north-west towards Chapman's Pool.

Plate 56. The inner end of the race off St Aldhelm's Head. The yacht on the right has just been through the race whereas the two yachts in the middle are taking the much smoother inshore passage.

worst with wind against tide; but it can be deceptively dangerous when there is a big residual swell running. This looks innocent enough until the odd wave suddenly builds up tremendously and then breaks. In bad weather one should avoid the race altogether by going outside it, but in good weather the inshore passage can be used (Plate 56). This is at times within 50m of the shore, and it is said, not quite correctly, that if the old coastguard position can be seen one should go closer in (Plate 57). Though the bottom shelves steeply down from the rocky shore, the strip of calm water is very narrow, leaving little margin for error; therefore it should be avoided during strong onshore winds even though part of the strength of the wind is lost under the cliffs. The rocks to watch out for when 'rounding tight', as they say locally, are on the point of the head, and a little to the east of the point of the head. There is also a rock close in on the west side called East Land Rock, awash at low water and far enough out for small fishing boats to go inside. As the name implies, it will be found when Anvil Light is just visible round the near cliff.

Plate 57. The coastguard lookout station viewed from the inshore passage.

Chapter 6

Chapman's Pool to Worbarrow Tout

On turning the corner to the north-west under the cliff, there is no escape from the contrary current which goes slack only briefly at high water. The valley that appears on the right, called Pier Bottom, leads up to the busy St Aldhelm's Quarry, the only remaining Purbeck quarry working Portland- type stone. Pier Bottom is so named as the St Aldhelm's Quarry stone used to go out by sea from a pier at the end of the valley, of which there is now no sign though odd lumps of dressed stone can be seen on the beach. There are off-lying rocks between Pier Bottom and Chapman's Pool, so it is not a place to hug the shore. For example, Liver Rock stands some little way offshore just north of the northerly point of Pier Bottom. Further north again of Pier Bottom below Emmett's Hill are two gaps in the rocks with beaches. (Plate 58). The southerly of these west-facing pebble coves is rather rocky but, on the rare occasions that the weather allows, it is easier to land at the Chapman's Pool end

Plate 58. Emmett's Hill. The north beach below the cliffs in shadow - as opposed to the smaller beach just to the right - generally has the easiest landing.

of the second, and more northerly cove One has to pick one's way through some bulky offlying rocks (Plate 59). It is an attractive place to anchor off and only occasionally do people come here via the shore. Paths can be taken to Chapman's Pool, and to Pier Bottom, from where one may, if feeling sufficiently energetic, ascend the 162 or so steps of Shar Point to the summit of St Aldhelm's Head.

Chapman's Pool (Plate 60) is a popular and attractive anchorage when the wind is offshore and the swell low. The yellow mooring of the range safety vessel, laid at Lat. 50°35'.4N, Long 2°04'.1W serves as a useful guide on the way in. One is safe in any wind direction between north and east, and at least two metres will be found in the centre. Most of the bottom is good holding on mud or sand, though anchors do occasionally catch a bit of a rock ledge extending from the west shore under Houns-tout (Plate 61). There are odd submerged prominent rocks on this ledge too.

One can land anywhere on the beach, or on the slip by the boathouse on the east side. This was originally built by the coastguards, and there was also a lifeboat station built in 1867 alongside the stream. Though there was a clear need for a lifeboat on this bit of coast, it was too far away for the crew to man in a hurry, and was soon discontinued. It is worth mentioning that land breezes, formed by cool air flowing down the valleys at night, do occur at Chapman's Pool, and at other similar places along the shore. They may be strong enough to cause insecure sails to flap and boats to tug heavily at their anchors.

There are some attractive and energetic walks from Chapman's Pool. Starting in the dell by the beach called Seven Wells Hollow, paths can be taken to Houns-tout - tout meaning 'lookout' - Emmett's Hill, Worth Matravers, and Pier Bottom, all of which on a clear day well repay the effort.

Heading west from Chapman's Pool demands careful attention, due to the presence of the Kimmeridge Ledges. A useful rule of

Plate 59. The north beach seen from sea level. There are several large rocks to look out for when approaching this beach from seaward.

58

Plate 60. Chapman's Pool looking east.

thumb in good visibility is to head south-west from the anchorage until the Worbarrow Tout headland is in line with the eastern point of Arish Mell, called Cover Hole, on 307°Mag. However, there is scope to sail inside this line, given settled good weather. Egmont's Bight is grey-featured, rocky and too shallow for deep-keeled yachts. When coming to Egmont's Bight from Chapman's Pool, a berth has to be given to the rocks lying off Hard Cove

Plate 61. Looking up at Houns-tout from within Chapman's pool.

Plate 62. Landing at Hard Cove is for the birds.

(Plate 62) and Egmont's Point. There are remains of a building on the point called the Powder House, which is thought to have been another gun battery position. In addition, there is a legend that a brass cannon lies in the sea below, not that divers have ever found anything. Hard Cove has two beaches both liberally sprinkled with offshore rocks and landing at either beach is very difficult.

The low plateau to the west of the point, with grass and shrubs, is quite a pleasant place to visit. Apparently the head of the cliff slipped down Houns-tout without disturbing the topsoil, allowing crops such as potatoes to flourish as at Ring-Bum Gardens. The lower plateau may have been called Molly's Garden, and the upper plateau is either called Cherry Garden, Grandmother's Garden or the Half Cliff. At one time the only road to Encombe was round the front of Houns-tout, having turned off the road going south from Kingston at Westhill Wood. After a landslide took the old road away, the present one was built through Quarry Wood.

The best way into Egmont Bight (Plate 63) is to nose cautiously in close to the rocks on the east side, aiming for the right hand end of the beach. The single rock shown on the chart is located by the cliffs in line on 285°Mag, and the larger of the streams wriggling down the cliff on 033°Mag, but there is more than this one rock. Moreover the bay becomes yet shallower to the west. The most convenient landing place in this remote spot is towards the east end of the beach where much flotsam

60

Plate 63. Egmont Bight looking east. Best landing for the intrepid is in the far corner of the bay.

accumulates. The rocks on the east side of the bay form a lagoon at low water with access from the north, known as Egmont Pond.

Behind the bluff at the west end of Egmont Bight there is another little beach where a waterfall tumbles down the cliff. This finely-pebbled cove is called Freshwater Steps (Plate 64). The freshwater stream comes down from Encombe, and at one

Plate 64. Freshwater Steps - which only go half way down the cliff. Remnants of the white marble continuation can be seen scattered on the beach.

Plate 65. Rope Lake Hole, an unusual anchorage between Shakes Head Ledge on the left and Rope Lake Ledge on the right.

time there were massive marble steps descending the cliff face built by Lord Eldon in the early 19th Century. No doubt as a result of some storm, the steps are now distributed over the smooth ledge in the approach to the beach. There are also foundations of a pump house, used to supply sea-water to Lord Eldon's large bath, which is still in place under the Encombe library floor. Access to the beach from the cliff top was once re-established by means of a ladder and scaffolding but this has now gone. Access from seaward requires one to pass over a succession of reefs and is inadvisable, except by dinghy at high tide in flat calm conditions.

From Chapman's Pool to Kimmeridge the cliffs are composed of crumbling blackstone shale, in complete contrast to the sturdy limestone of the 'Back of the Cliff'. One does not have to stand long on the beach before hearing the clatter of a cliff fall, a telling reminder that it would be rash to climb or sit under most parts of these unstable cliffs.

There is a famous wreck half a mile south of Freshwater Steps, shown as awash on the chart. This is the *Treveal*, which went aground on 9 January 1920, returning from her maiden voyage to

Calcutta carrying a cargo of jute and manganese ore. As she started to break up in a gale her crew took to the lifeboats, with the loss of 36 out of the 43 people on board. Later a drifter called the *Abide* was beached after being holed on the wreck when trying to salvage the manganese ore, and a ship called the *Glenmore* also hit the remains of the *Treveal* and sank. Subsequently Trinity House had the wrecks and 2000 tons of manganese ore flattened, and there is a good seven metres over them now.

More of a problem to fishing boats is the cargo of a stone barge which sank in shallow water some quarter of a mile north-west of the *Treveal*. The large lumps of stone dry at low water springs.

To the west of Freshwater Steps, there is a concentration of south-east pointing ledges clearly visible from the cliff path below Eldon Seat. They are at best thinly covered, and this is no place to be in bad weather; but in calm, settled conditions enterprising navigators will find an unusual anchorage 0.2nm east of Rope Lake Head, called Rope Lake Hole (Plate 65). To get there one should steer for Rope Lake Head from the direction of St Aldhelm's Head. In the approach to the bay, appropriately called Deepwater, a line should be picked up such that one is on a course of 325°Mag when pointing at a pyramid of scree descending from a ravine half way up the cliff, with a jumble of light coloured rocks along its base. This course leads between Rope Lake Ledge to the west and Shakes Head Ledge to the east. When the tide is running and the sea smooth, guidance will be given by the tide rip over Rope Lake Ledge. There is a flat bottom at The Hole and three metres of water quite close to the shore. The best landing place is just to the west of the scree.

Many more ledges exist between Rope Lake Head and Kimmeridge Bay, with a surprising old landing place in between them called Clavell's Hard (Plate 66). It was from here that the entrepreneurial Sir William Clavell shipped alum in the early 17th Century. It was also a centre of the shale mine industry, active in the mid 19th Century. It seems that there used to be huts on the cliff and on the beach,.

At low water spring tide it is possible to walk along the base of the cliffs from Clavell's Hard to Kimmeridge. The Hard is not easy to reach by sea, unless it is very calm, owing to Grey Ledge and numerous lesser ledges; moreover there are large lumps of dressed rectangular stone on the grey rock floor in the approach, possibly part of the old pier. There is further evidence of the pier

Plate 66. The beach in the centre of the picture is called Clavell's Hard and once had a pier.

Plate 67. Clavell's Hard from sea level.

in the form of circular recesses in the rock floor, which are thought once to have taken the bases for the pier legs. Moreover the ledge has been cut away to give more depth for the flat-bottomed barges which were thought to have been used here to carry away Kimmeridge coal (Plate 67). Once ashore there is not much to see, except a heap of flotsam in the corner of the cliff, though not long ago tunnel openings could be seen in the cliff face. At the west end of the beach, a short steep climb up the lower cliff used to bring one onto a path leading to the top. With ongoing erosion the path disappeared over the cliff edge in early 1995.

A stream flows down to another private bay west of The Hard, with a similar flat grey floor of rock, imprinted by fossils. There are many healthy plant specimens of wild sea cabbage growing along this part of the cliff, as at several other places in the area. Given adequate soil, one might expect such plants to grow well, as strong winds are deflected upwards short of the face of the cliff, and they benefit from the tremendous sun trap. In addition to the sea cabbage, rock pipits and oystercatchers abound on this part of the coast.

Heading west, the outermost dangers to be avoided before getting to Kimmeridge Bay are Grey Ledge then Yellow Ledge. Beyond Yellow Ledge there are smaller ledges, the last one before the bay being known as Saucy Jack. Above these ledges stands the dark and brooding Hencliff, surmounted by the conspicuous Clavell's Tower, a 19th Century folly, thought to have been intended as a day-mark or lookout (Plate 68). The lighter-coloured strata in the cliffs that slope gently eastwards are limestone, and these provide the stronger structure which prevents the soft shale from crumbling faster than it does already. The alternating darkish shale and yellowish limestone is called Kimmeridge Clay, and was laid down on the seabed some 135 million years ago. Such formation known by the same name

Plate 68. The Hencliff and Clavell's Tower.

Plate 69. Kimmeridge Bay looking south-east.

is quite common elsewhere in the world and provides the essential soil for the Chablis vine. Weathering has given Hencliff a streamlined form, looking from westward rather like a giant upside-down ship. There is a concentration of slim natural ledges off Hencliff, and the remains of a stone pier at the west end constructed by the Wanostrocht company, one of many firms which tried to exploit the oil-bearing shale in the 19th Century without much success. The shale oil has a high sulphur content. When burnt, it gives off much smoke and a strong smell, so was found to be less satisfactory than coal. What has been a success though, is BP's oil well at Gaulter Gap on the top of the cliffs at the south-west end of the bay. This well, which was sunk in 1959, produces high quality oil in quantities only exceeded onshore in Britain by Wytch Farm. It should have run dry by now, so it must be fed from an unknown field.

Kimmeridge is a popular base for windsurfers, and divers whose inflatable craft arrive in large numbers during the summer (Plate 69). The slipway is steep, rather hard on motor car clutches, and not easy at low tide. Nevertheless, there is nowhere else more satisfactory to launch between Swanage and Weymouth (Plate 70). Thus there are plenty of weekenders in fine weather, but probably nothing like as many people about as there would have been in the early 19th Century when the shale, glass, alum and cement works were in full swing.

The bay is wide and shallow with red 8 knot speed limit buoys laid between Clavell's Tower, and Broad Bench Point on the other side of the bay. It is exposed to the south, allowing a swell to come in. Nevertheless, as the water is clear, the bay is often busy with divers and snorkelers in summer, so care needs to be taken in the approaches.

Kimmeridge is the eastern limit of the Lulworth sea danger area, and therefore firing schedules ought to be determined before going further west, (see Chapter 12). Thus it may make a convenient stopping place when the sea is calm, whilst waiting to visit one of the places within the danger zone. The only beaches in the range area which are officially open to the public during non-firing periods are Worbarrow Bay and Charnel, and then only after they have been checked to be clear of unexploded munitions.

If exploring the bay itself one will first find Maple Ledge in the east corner of the bay. Then comes Washing Ledge, the longest of the several fingers of rock running from the middle of the beach out into the bay, and finally The Flats under the BP oil well. An isolated rock exists to the south of Washing Ledge, called Devil's Rock, or sometimes Almond's Rock. This is exposed towards low water, and one can walk out to it on an exceptionally low tide.

There have been two lifeboats at Kimmeridge, both called *Mary Heape*. The initial five-oared boat first saw service in 1872 and was replaced by a ten-oared boat before the station was closed down in 1896.

Plate 70. The slipway at Kimmeridge.

Plate 71. Hobarrow Bay, Broadbench Point, Charnel Bay and Kimmeridge Bay.

Plate 72. Long Ebb Ledge in the foreground extends to seaward well beyond what can be seen.

When Kimmeridge was thought to be a burgeoning mineral centre, the Gaulter cottages were built to house the work force, with the intention of adding further parallel lines of cottages later. As none of the enterprises lasted long, only the one line of cottages was ever built. The coastal path passes between the cliff and the south end of the cottages, where a small German mine, caught in fishing nets in 1951, is to be seen.

Westwards by sea from Kimmeridge Bay to within the sea danger area, there is an inlet before the point called Charnel, where there used to be boat sheds and the lifeboat house. This site was no doubt chosen because the water is deeper in the approaches and there is more protection from the west. No sign of boat sheds exist now, but at the corner of the bay, between the wide ledge to the east and the rocks to the west, there is a clean approach to the beach and a path up to the cliff top which is closed when the range is active.

Broad Bench Point is presumably named after the wide flat ledge on the promontory, where there used to be a coastguard lookout position. Though the ledge ends abruptly, giving an impression of deep water off its end, this is not so and it should be given a wide berth.

The next bay is Hobarrow (Plate 71) which, though pleasant in its way and apparently a site of Roman industry, has a rather barren aspect and no access to the cliff top. Up to three metres can be found within 100m of the cliff, and there are patches of sand between the kelp on which to anchor, if stopping for a meal or a swim in settled weather. Before the establishment of the range, the best landing point near high water would have been alongside the ledge close to the shore. Everywhere else is rocky at low water.

Long Ebb ledge (Plate 72) is the aptly named underwater spit to the west of Hobarrow Bay. It consists of a steep ledge running deceptively far out offshore to the south-west. It can be avoided by keeping Clavell's Tower well open on the steep cliff at Broad Bench Point. Moreover one should keep on west, and not be tempted into Brandy Bay until the point where the vegetation comes right down to the sea is well past the beam.

Brandy Bay, though completely exposed to swell and the prevailing wind, makes a lovely out of the way anchorage when conditions are suitable (Plate 73). The variety in the overhanging 130m high Gadcliff, which towers over the bay, comes from the

Plate 73. The Gadcliff overlooking Brandy Bay in morning light.

Plate 74. Patches of sand off the Gadcliff can be found for the anchor. The only obvious beach is to the right of the lone offshore rock in the centre of the picture.

layering of its strata of Purbeck Beds, Portland Stone, Portland Sand then Kimmeridge Clay and Shale. Peregrine falcons and ravens nest in the crags of the cliff, and the partially-wooded middle slopes support flowers, butterflies, foxes, black faced sheep and goats. Surprisingly, it once had a Roman settlement; and not so surprisingly, given the remoteness and name, it was once a smugglers' haunt.

Deep water, and sandy strips on which to anchor, can be found close to the shore, opposite a small beach to the east of a collection of large rocks on the water's edge, with one offshore loner (Plate 74). Approach should be from the south before anchoring in three to four metres of water. There is an off-lying reef some 30m off this small beach, and at low water the evenly-exposed rock tops are arrayed like soldiers' helmets. It is interesting to speculate where the smugglers could have landed in the past. It would have been difficult to land on this beach at night, to say the least, but there are two other tiny beaches further to the east with slightly easier approaches. The first, and most likely, is below a distinctive triangular rock perched on the undercliff. The channel between overhanging dark yellowish rocks is not much wider than a sheep dip and is hard to find, but brings one to a clean, smooth, grey-bouldered beach (Plate 75). The second, though having a much wider entry between high black craggy rocks, has one or two rocks at the landing point and less offshore depth, as the eastern end of Brandy Bay is all shallow parallel reefs. Past these, on the way to the beach at the north-east end of the bay, spherical black rocks will be found, of

Plate 75. The sheep-dip beach.

about the size of the mine at Gaulter - i.e. about a metre in diameter, and smooth boulders stratified in several hues of colour.

Those landing anywhere at Brandy Bay might like to know that, in addition to the danger of unexploded munitions, adders are said to dwell under the Gadcliff, as well as the other flora and fauna. Moreover the highly inclined upward traverse from the beach to the cliff path leading to Kimmeridge must in places test even the goats.

At the most southerly point of the Gadcliff shoreline further to the west, one will come across what was once a magnificent lump of cliff top, known as the Wagon Rock (Plate 77). Though this is prominently marked on the chart, it has split in several directions and may soon become much like all other nearby rocks. As part of Purbeck Marine Wildlife Reserve, a scientific area in the form of a box has been established from Wagon Rock to one kilometre seaward, extending either side from Broad Bench to Worbarrow Tout. The aim is to maintain a marine area with as little human interference as possible. The area has no legal status and relies on voluntary agreement with passers-by. After the discovery of seven sea horses off the Dorset coast in 1995 it is possible that these and other species may re-establish themselves, given such opportunities.

The shore to the west of Wagon Rock is sometimes called Wagon Bay (Plate 78). This leads to the recess in the cliff called Pondfield (Plate 79). There are numerous rocks, large and small, inside the headlands of this little bay, probably making

Plate 76. Brandy Bay is clear and clean.

Plate 77. Wagon Rock in the foreground. The dark coloured ground behind the rock is Kimmeridge Coal.

Plate 78. Wagon Bay shags taking flight.

Plate 79. Pondfield from sea level.

Plate 80. The east end of Worbarrow Bay with Worbarrow Tout in the foreground.

unnecessary the wartime anti-invasion dragon's teeth still to be seen above the shore. Pondfield has attractive rock formation and a cave on the east side, but with so many large submerged rocks it is more of a place for divers than for boats. Better possibilities exist to the north after rounding Worbarrow Tout (Plate 80) and the reef on its western tip.

Plate 81. Worbarrow Tout looking east and the rock-strewn Pondfield behind. The road leads to Tynham Village.

Chapter 7

Worbarrow Bay to White Nothe

Worbarrow is an outstandingly beautiful deep-water bay, ringed by cliffs of wealden marl and sandstone which, after rain, can glow with red, orange, yellow and purple when the sun is low in the west. A great advantage of Worbarrow is that, by selecting the appropriate end, shelter can be found when winds are from the south-west, and through north to south-east. Worbarrow was another site of Roman activity, and at the eastern corner there are more recent remains of a stone slipway with fishermen's and coastguards' cottages. The old coastguard lookout position was appropriately on top of the Tout (Plate 81) where, long ago, there used to be a flagstaff and signalling cannon. The east end of the bay can be quite sheltered (Plate 82), with some protection from the south if well tucked in. Nevertheless the beach can get crowded, even at night by fishermen, and is subject to disturbance from land breezes which drain down the valley at night. When the swell is not running one can land on the sandy beach, or upon a collection of concrete dragon's teeth lying on their sides. A ten minute walk brings one to the interesting derelict village of Tyneham, deserted since the extension of the Lulworth range in 1940. A visit to the church

Plate 82. The east end of Worbarrow Bay is a delightful anchorage in calm weather. The humps on the skyline above the mast are Flowers Barrow.

Plate 83. Mupe Bay.

and schoolhouse will supply much information about the locality, including, for example, details of Flowers Barrow, the iron age hill fort overlooking the bay from Rings Hill.

The chart shows a clean shore at the north-east end of Worbarrow Bay, and this beach is used occasionally by Service landing craft. From Cow Corner to Cover Hole, the eastern promontory of Arish Mell Gap, odd submerged rocks extend nearly 200m out. The shallow inlet of Arish Mell Gap, with its white sandy beach, has as its centre piece a pipeline from Winfrith Heath nuclear power station. The outlet is marked by a yellow lit buoy two miles out to sea, the so-called Atomic Buoy, which is used by the Weymouth sailing clubs as a racing mark. West from Arish Mell there are several offshore rocks up to 300m offshore. Thus it may pay to keep outside a line between Cover Hole and Mupe Rocks. The promontory half way between Barber's Rock and Mackerel Rock inside this line is called Cockpit, and just east of it lies Black Rock.

Plate 84. Mupe Rocks from the south-east.

The west end of Worbarrow is called Mupe Bay (Plate 83), locally Mupes Bay, where good protection can be found from the prevailing wind and swell, not much of which finds its way round Mupe Rocks. The expanse of white cliff created by recent huge landslides makes for easy identification from offshore, and approach should be from the south-east. There is deep water close in to the western beach, and one can be comfortable at Mupe even in force seven from the west, but a riding light is recommended as fishing boats come in for shelter at night. Steps lead up to Bindon Hill, once called Swines Back, where there is the offer of a circuitous walk to Lulworth, starting either by the upper route via the 12th Century chapel-cum-cottage at Little Bindon, or along the cliff via the fossil forest.

In spite of the fact that Worbarrow Bay is obviously a breached wall on a larger scale than Lulworth Cove, not much ledge is left underwater; so the most easterly of the Mupe Rocks, called End Rock, is not far short of the end of the hazards of the point (Plate 84). However, the large-scale chart does show one 2.8m patch 200m to the east of it, which of course most craft will get over in safety.

The Mupe Rocks (Plate 85) are enjoyable to explore by dinghy in tranquil weather, when one can be assured of the company of a good assembly of shags. The eastern lagoon looks tempting as

Plate 85. Mupe Bay, Mupe Rocks and the Bacon Hole. Submerged rocks can be seen on the seaward side of the Mupe Rocks. On the other hand the dark patch further out and to the left is the shadow of the photographic helicopter.

Plate 86. The Bacon Hole, showing the rocks.

Plate 87. The Bacon Hole seen from ground level. The best anchorage is on the far side, just to the right of the lower cave.

a shoal-draft anchorage, but has a profusion of shallow reefs. A small pool can be found just inside the lagoon when leaving Arish Rock, the centremost of the larger rocks, to starboard.

Going into the initially deep inlet to the east of the largest of Mupe Rocks, one will come to a sill of about one metre, before slightly deeper water in the pool beyond. An old engraving gives the names of the larger central group of rocks, from east to west, as Slip rock, Arish rock and Wreckneck rock. The only deep semi-sheltered spot to be found is at the most westerly of the pools of the Bacon Hole, perhaps named after an alleged bygone 'Bacon House' on the cliff top shown in the engraving, or after the streaky formation of the rock (Plate 86). One should keep to the west in the narrow entrance to avoid the large rock in the middle, then turn to port where there is a small pool of three to four metres. In the west corner of the bay a pair of celebrated smuggler's caves can be seen, believed to have been put to regular use in the 19th Century (Plate 87).

The long straight weatherworn Purbeck stone buttress called The Southcliff, but known to geologists as a fine example of 'broken beds', (Plate 88) can be approached to within 50m, and much closer in most parts. Potter's Hole, shown on the chart, is a cavity near the top of the cliff where, supposedly, a Mr Potter once lived.

Plate 88. The Southcliff.

Plate 89. Lulworth Cove can get a little crowded. Note the sandy patches to the north of the Range Safety Vessel buoy and the ledge at the western side of the entrance.

Plate 90. The Stairhole can be seen in the centre of the picture.

Lulworth Cove (Plate 89) is a pleasant anchorage in fair weather. It can make a convenient point to wait for access to anchorages within the sea danger area, and is too well known to warrant detailed guidance. Suffice to say that one should tend to the east of the entrance to avoid a ledge, sometimes called The Rat, making due allowance for the cross tide. One can expect to find a swell and swirling gusts which come round the north of Hambury Tout when the wind has any south in it and is above Force 4. Moreover one should be prepared to leave before any severe weather arrives from this direction. The best anchorage for visitors is on the sandy bottom, not far to the north-east of the range safety vessel's yellow and black buoy. The concrete ramp on the west side of the bay is too short to use as a slip, besides which the access road is closed for much of the time during the summer. There is an 8 knot speed limit in the cove.

Stairhole is the first point of interest west of Lulworth (Plate 90), particularly on the inside, where some amazing crumpled Purbeck stone strata can be seen. The open entrance on the west side is best approached from the south by dinghy along the east wall, thence inside to a shallow rocky pool (Plate 91). Alternatively, having avoided a large submerged rock south of the entrance, one can get in by the west archway which has deep water through to another rather deeper pool on the inside. Finally, there is the larger eastern archway with a deep water passage going through to yet another unconnected pool on the inside. This is the easiest way into the Stairhole, with more room

Plate 91. The Stairhole seen from seaward.

to turn (Plate 92). However, apart from the crumpled Purbeck strata, and giving minor excitement to holiday swimmers when arriving through the cavern entrance, Stairhole has not much to recommend it to mariners. Landing there on the boulders is difficult, and there is evidence of a nearby sewer outfall, not that the holiday swimmers seem to take much notice.

Proceeding again westwards towards Dungy Head, the offshore rocks around Church Rocks and the Ballstone can be avoided by keeping the flagpole on the east side of Lulworth in line. If not heeding this clearing transit, it should be remembered that there are submerged rocks some 25m to the south-east of the Ballstone. Incidentally, old photographs show the Ballstone as a perfectly spherical dome, doubtless accounting for its name.

On the east side of Dungy Head there is a cove which some maps call Dungy Beach. This is not what most people would call a beach, more a rocky indentation with a steepish cliff behind, too rocky and unsheltered to warrant investigation by boat.

Around the corner one can see into St Oswald's Bay (Plate 93) where a reef continues west for some 150m, a little inside the line of the cliff. The salient feature of the reef is Pinion Rock which is not normally covered (Plate 94). As the reef extends inshore, the whole east end of the bay should be avoided; but if one comes in opposite the ravine up on the cliff, mid-way between Norman and Pinion Rocks, two or three metres of water will be found close up to the beach. The bottom is mainly covered in seaweed, with odd patches of sand on which to anchor, assuming the weather allows the use of this exposed situation.

Plate 92. The view from beneath the easternmost arch of The Stairhole.

Plate 93. *The rocky east end of St Oswald's Bay from above. Pinion Rock is the nearest of the bunch on the left.*

Plate 94. *The rocky east end of St Oswald's Bay viewed from sea level. Pinion Rock is on the right and the Ballstone can be seen off Dungy Head in the background.*

Plate 95. Man o'War Cove.

Beyond Norman Rock lies Man o'War Cove (Plate 95). It is not for deep-keeled yachts, but makes an attractive picnic anchorage for shoal-draft boats. Approach should be from the south towards the widest gap in the line of rocks running east from Durdle Door Point. The entrance has an even depth of at least one metre at chart datum, with more depth inside the bay to the west. Therefore, after entering, one needs to turn sharply to port and head briefly for the vertical stratum beside the steps, until opposite the rock forming the port side of the entrance. It does not pay to go further as the same vertical stratum extends eastwards underwater. The cove becomes gradually shallower elsewhere. Dinghies can get alongside the Man o'War Rock at the extreme north-west end, and the best landing point is on the north-west part of the beach, not far from the bottom of the steps. Such a sunny, attractive and sheltered spot is inevitably well populated in summer, especially with a large caravan site on the hill nearby (Plate 96).

On the other side of the peninsula to Man o'War Cove is the famous Durdle Door archway of highly inclined Portland stone, forming one of the best known features of the Dorset coast. There is deep water inside the archway which can be fun to visit when it is sheltered, but the remains of the breached Portland stone cliff form a three-quarter mile reef to the west requiring careful navigation. The best eastern gap is just east of the middle point between Durdle Door (Plate 97) and Bull Rock, and though the reef varies a bit in height, there should be three metres over it at high water, except close in to Durdle Door where, at about six

Plate 96. Man o' War Cove from cliff level, looking eastwards.

Plate 97. Durdle Door and Bull Rock. A submerged rock called The Frenchman can just be seen off Durdle Door. The valley beyond Bull Rock is called Scratchy Bottom.

Plate 98. Durdle Door.

metres distance, there is a rock called The Frenchman, about a metre below the surface at low water. Craft without masts drawing less than half a metre can go through the door itself (Plate 98). There is plenty of depth on either side, but not much over the threshold. Even with the right sort of vessel, one should choose high water and calm conditions. The most sheltered spot for landing is towards the east end of the steep beach of fine shingle. There are rocks at the extreme end.

Rather than tuck oneself in by Durdle Door, which may be rather crowded, deep water and a rock-free shore can be found just west of the dip appearing in the cliffs, called Scratchy Bottom. One should not go close to the pinnacle Butter Rock as there are rocks all around it. Moreover to seaward the Blind Cow (often covered), and the Cow and the Calf mark high points on the ledge, needing due caution (Plate 99). One of the deepest routes over the ledge, with up to seven metres, is mid-way between the Cow and the Calf (Plate 100). The flood tide runs strongly through the gap. It is possible to avoid the ledge altogether by approaching from the west, but initial entry from any direction to the north of the ledge, sometimes known as Durdle Cove, should be attempted for the first time in a deep-keeled yacht only in settled weather.

Bat's Head is shallow on either side, and it is possible to walk through Bat's Hole, sometimes known as the Eye of The Monster, at low tide (Plate 101). There is a mile of beach between Bat's Head and White Nothe called Middle Bottom (Plate 102). With no shelter from the south it is not often the place to visit, but in calm conditions it makes a good anchorage with plenty of room for all. The shingle beach is steep-to, and is generally quite deserted as there is no access from Chaldon Down above, but a ledge lies off it in much of the middle part, making landing difficult. In addition, when approaching from the

Plate 99. Bat's Head. The breaking water marks The Calf on the left and The Cow on the right. The submerged ledge can be seen to the right of The Cow.

Plate 100. The view from the passage between The Cow and The Calf. The Cow is on the right.

Plate 101. A distant view of Greenhill, Weymouth seen through Bat's Hole. Butter Rock is on the right.

Plate 102. Looking east along Middle Bottom beach.

east, allowance should be made for the submerged ledge on the west side of the Calf.

Towards the west end of Middle Bottom the white cliffs become higher and more dramatic, and the shore more rocky (Plate 103). There are some attractive coves between the rocks, though the beaches are rather uncomfortably narrow. In very settled weather it is another place for anchoring offshore and landing by dinghy.

Just to the east of the magnificent great promontory of White Nothe (Plate 104) there is a particularly delightful landing place called Angel Bay (Plate 105) where the beach is much wider than at Middle Bottom. The best point to land is in the middle (Plate 106).

When passing the point of The Nothe, where there is an even horizontal pattern in the chalk of the lowest face, one should keep a little offshore, and be wary of the rock shown on the chart as The Bear, to be found 300m west of the tip of The Nothe. Moreover The Bear has a number of inshore attendants not shown on the chart. Before getting to The Bear there is another possible landing place, Ochre Bay, (Plate 107) about 150m west of The Nothe with a very rocky approach encouraging the use of oars (Plate 108). One may have to share this beach with the odd naturist couple, who have clambered round from where the cliff path comes near the shore. Another pebble beach to the east of Ochre Bay, backed by green scrub and ivy and known as Bushy Bay, is accessible by steps from the path from the top of the cliff and from Ringstead Bay along the shore, but not from seaward. Rocks lie a short way offshore from The Bear to the beach at Ringstead.

Plate 103. The high chalk cliffs to the east of White Nothe.

Plate 104. White Nothe viewed from the south-east.

Plate 105. White Nothe and Angel Bay.

Plate 106. Angel Bay.

Plate 107. The west side of White Nothe where the only relatively rock free place for landing, Ochre Bay, can be seen just left of the centre. The Zig Zag path can be seen in places on White Nothe.

Plate 108. Ochre Bay.

Plate 109. Bags Hole from the air.

Plate 110. Bags Hole from sea level.

Chapter 8

Ringstead Bay to Weymouth

The east end of the finely-pebbled Ringstead Bay, known by some as Bag's Hole (Plate 109) after a well-known fisherman who was drowned at this spot, is quite deep with 3m of water close to the shore (Plate 110). As it is easily accessible from The Creek caravan site, one will not be alone here for long in the holiday season. A round walk can be taken from Ringstead Bay up the path to the diminutive wooden St Catherine's Church, past Holworth House to the top of White Nothe, down the smugglers' path, known also as The Zig Zag, and back along the undercliff. It is a glorious walk on a dry day when the paths are not slippery, and the wooded dells of the undercliff will be found to have a semi-tropical micro-climate.

Maps show a spot described as Burning Cliff, and this alludes to an event in 1826 when something caused the oil shale to ignite, which then continued to smoulder on for some years afterwards. Of more immediate interest to sailors are what the locals logically call Ringstead Ledges (Plate 111), which are not quite the ledges off Bran Point as named on the chart. The proper Ringstead Ledges are shown on the chart as unnamed offshore ledges

Plate 111. Ringstead Ledges, looking north.

opposite the buildings at Ringstead. The two reefs are in the form of two fish meeting head to head. The eastern ledge is called Peter Pan, which partly dries at low water, and the higher western one is just called 'The Ledge'. The easiest entry is from the east. When approaching the western entrance one needs to skirt around the outer reef and, once in the channel, one needs to stay on the reef side, rather than the shore. The shallowest entry of the three is between the two ledges as there is a narrow ledge connecting both main ledges. Twin-keeled yachts have been known to use this channel at high water springs but it is usually only suitable for dinghies. Marginally the deepest point is opposite the white house called The Creek. The ledges provide protection for privately-laid summer boat moorings in the deep lagoon where big fronds of seaweed grow, and provide winter windsurfers with some shelter for launching (Plate 112). The outer ends of the reef can be difficult to locate, and the south-east point has been known to cause problems, but there are usually lobster pot floats out on the ledges which help to indicate their whereabouts. It is tempting to anchor clear of the moorings between the reefs and the shore. However the holding is bad owing to the abundance of seaweed, and at night the offshore breeze could easily cause an anchored craft to drag onto the reef.

Beach replenishment was undertaken at Ringstead at the end of 1995 and a short rock groyne has been constructed at the eastern end of the caravan park which slightly narrows the passage between the beach and Peter Pan. The beach is steep and there is a rough track between the beach houses down to the shingle.

Less than half a mile to the west there are more reefs all round and well offshore of Bran Point (Plate 113), so this is definitely a place to avoid in bad weather. Moreover the ribs and jagged pieces of the coal barge *Minx*, which lost her mooring in a storm

Plate 112. The lagoon inside Ringstead Ledges, looking east.

Plate 113. Bran Point with its maze of offshore ledges showing below the surface. The Upton Fort gun battery is at one o'clock from the building on top of the cliffs.

in 1927, lie on the part of the Pool Ledge which the locals call West Maze and are a salutary reminder of what lies underneath (Plate 114). Nevertheless, if circumstances allow one to land to the west of Perry Ledge - or Crooked Ledge as they call it locally - there is a pretty beach to be found. It is at the point on the chart where a wreck is shown on the shore 100m east of Bran Point. An approach should be made from the east, and at low water some protection can be given by the ledge which acts like a breakwater owing to what the geologists call the Bran Point Fault. As a result of the fault, the Pool Ledges with Frenchman's Ledge inside, are a different form of rock to Bran and Perry Ledge. Half a mile south of Bran Point, the Weymouth Sailing Club lays a racing mark in summer, painted with an 'R' - for Ringstead.

Plate 114. Bran Point viewed from the west. The structure on the left is part of the wreck of the Minx.

Plate 115. The ledges at Osmington Mills.

Another obstacle to inshore pilotage, Hannah's Ledge, not shown on the chart, lies between Pool Ledge and Osmington Mills waterfall. The privately-owned Upton Fort, which is marked on the chart, can also be seen in Plate 113. It was built in 1902 as a site for two 9.2in breech-loading guns to complement the heavy defences of Portland Harbour, and remained operational until the end of the Second World War.

The only way through the rocky approach at Osmington (Plate 115) is from the west, between outer and inner parallel ledges in the form of a dock. Osmington Mills was the landing place for the very successful smuggler Pierre La Tour, known as 'French Peter', and it is conceivable that these ledges were used for

Plate 116. The slipway at Osmington Mills.

unloading contraband in the late 18th Century from his cutter *L'Hirondelle*. The steep privately-owned slipway (Plate 116) was built long ago by coastguards and in World War II was used for a lifeboat. Since the war, the slip has been used for small fishing boats, but not so often nowadays, as access through the rocks is difficult even when it is calm. Moreover present day fishermen prefer big powerful vessels giving them a wide area of operation. In the 19th Century fishing boats used to operate from the beach to the west of Osmington known locally as Tank Bay, and the beach can make a good landing spot in settled weather. A bizarre hazard to contend with in this bay is the open end of a 12cm cladded steel pipe which emerges at low water from the sea bed, pointing roughly north-west (Plate 117). If White Nothe is in sight off Bran Point one is about 100m clear of the pipe; if not, one has to keep a good look out.

Plate 117. The Osmington Mills pipe.

Black Head Ledges run in narrow parallel bands, which make landing difficult over much of the length of Osmington Bay or Short Lake as it is known locally. Once over the ledge there is a calm strip, sometimes used by fishermen as a sheltered

Plate 118. Redcliffe Point.

waterway. The bay can be crowded in summer as a Pontin's holiday centre is just behind the beach.

Redcliff Point (Plate 118) is an attractive headland at the end of the bay where erosion of Oxford clay has formed patterns in the cliff, and where bushy vegetation provides cover for wildlife. At the point itself a reef curls eastward. This makes a shallow sandy dinghy harbour, the inside of which is nicely sheltered except at high water when the reef is covered, and when the wind is in the east. A triangle of three rocks awash at chart datum lie 300m east of the reef. They are not easy to locate unless marked by a lobster pot buoy, as often occurs.

There is a gap called Broad Rock where dinghies can get in at high water on the west side of Redcliff Point, and odd offshore rocks appear between Broad Rock and Bowleaze Cove. The cove has a concrete slip which is good at high water and can be used by arrangement with the holiday camp. In addition, there is a small pier at Bowleaze which is mainly of use to jet skiers, who have a prescribed operating area off the cove. On the west side of Bowleaze under Furzy Cliff there is a submerged wall, not shown on the chart, made with lumps of Portland stone to protect the cliffs from erosion (Plate 119). It starts at Bowleaze, and runs in an unbroken line parallel to the shore, until a point opposite the most southerly block of new flats at Overcombe. In summer orange buoys may be laid to mark the western extremity of the wall. In addition, between May and October, round white 0.6m diameter 8 knot speed limit buoys are laid 200m offshore between Bowleaze and Weymouth harbour. Within this line of buoys bathers, water skiers, water bikers and windsurfers have prescribed areas.

Plate 119. The north end of Weymouth Bay and Bowleaze Cove showing the submerged wall.

Plate 120. Weymouth Harbour entrance.

Not far from where the chart shows a 0.9m drying rock off Overcombe, which used to be marked with a post, there is a wide channel for windsurfers marked by speed limit buoys. Further south, off Greenhill, there is also a wide gap in the speed limit area, marked by dan-buoys with appropriate port and starboard topmarks, to give access to water ski boats. A large shingle groyne was constructed off Greenhill in 1995 with the intention of keeping in place the pebbles recently used to replenish Preston beaches, rather than having them move south with wave action and the general anti-clockwise current in the bay. Southwards from Greenhill one comes to Weymouth's main bathing beaches which become progressively flatter, wider and of finer sand towards the harbour. Just north of the harbour entrance (Plate 120) there is a well-established yacht anchorage, known by some as Dicky Bird, and this, too, is the area where the Weymouth Sailing Club start their races. Holding ground is good, though the swell can come round the corner. There are landing steps on the seaward side of the North Pier, or one can land on the beach.

The Harbourmaster has a patrol boat for Weymouth Bay. It is a 4.5m white Ski Doo waterjet capable of 30 knots and marked 'Harbour Authority' in lifeboat orange letters.

Plate 121. Weymouth Harbour, Weymouth Beach and Radipole Lake.

Weymouth's popularity as a seaside resort stems from the patronage of King George III and his family 200 years ago. The King, who was unattired, first took to the water from a bathing machine in 1789. Use of bathing machines remained popular up to the turn of the 19th Century and thereafter, it is said, their wheels were removed and they were sold off as allotment huts.

Weymouth harbour (Plate 121) fulfils many needs for the yachtsman. As the only sheltered harbour for many miles in either direction, it makes a natural port of call for those on passage. Moreover it has charm, a friendly nature, easy access, alongside berthing, free showers and free power supplies, so it attracts seagoing visitors in its own right. The railway and bus services can be useful too.

Before entering the harbour one should refer to the almanac regarding the traffic light system displayed from a mast on the south pier. The lights are used to control shipping in the entrance when, for example, Channel Island ferries, which are particularly busy in summer, are entering or leaving harbour. The most remarkable ferries are the Condor wave-piercers which are an impressive sight, both in the harbour and in the open sea at their service speed of 35 knots. Considering their bulk and power their wash is remarkably little, however, for small craft it has still has to be reckoned with.

The harbour is formed from the lower reach of the Wey River and is therefore long and narrow. The harbour master (Channel 12) will usually direct visiting yachts over 10m to Customs House Quay on the north side of the harbour, and yachts under 10m to Cove Row on the south side of the harbour. The north side has the showers, power points and Weymouth Chandlery whereas the south side has the attractions of the lively Hope Square and Brewers Quay. One can, of course, get from one side to the other by means of the opening Town Bridge, above which many local boats lie, or by means of the cross-harbour ferry, located down river towards the ferry terminal.

There are two local eventualities which deserve mention. Firstly, from time to time fishing competitions take place from Weymouth Harbour with the rule that no competing vessel leaves before a given time, usually 9 am. If happening to be near the harbour entrance at this moment, non-fishing mariners could be taken aback by a swarm of accelerating vessels intent upon their objective. The second small matter regards the harbour master's staff, who, very reasonably, use a loud hailer to give instructions to incoming craft should they have failed to have fully slowed down on arrival. When the volume control is set to maximum in quiet conditions, the unexpected and commanding voice from on high is enough to make any sailor jump out of his yellow wellies.

Continuing south from Weymouth Harbour, the drying rock called the Mixen and a rocky shoreline will be found under the Nothe between the northern arm of Portland Harbour breakwater and Newton's Cove. The Nothe provides the site for a large fort built in 1860 as part of the defences of Portland Harbour. Newton's Cove (Plate 122) has a 6 knot speed limit and is well sheltered from the west. Though they are within the marked DG Range cable area, small craft do anchor close in where they are clear of seabed cables. The cove has a rocky landing and steps up to the coastal path.

Plate 122. Newton's Cove.

Chapter 9

Portland Harbour

Portland Harbour is a large area of sheltered sea with space for many activities. Unlike most sea ports which have developed in a river estuary Portland Harbour is an enclosed bay. Thus there is a demand for Portland Harbour water for aquariums due to its clarity and ocean-like quality. Generally there is an anti-clockwise direction to the current within the harbour, with outgoing tidal streams of up to a knot at the two north entrances and maybe three knots at the South Ship Channel. The shallower north and west parts of the harbour tend to be used for yacht moorings and leisure activities, whereas the deeper south and east parts of the harbour were dominated by the Royal Navy until the closure of the naval base in 1995. The Naval Air Station is still in use and there is still some other naval activity outside the harbour, details of which will be found in Chapter 12. With a two-mile fetch within the harbour a choppy sea can develop, so any leeward end of Portland Harbour does not provide a comfortable anchorage.

The future manager of the old naval base is likely to be a commercial organisation which may be expected to develop the facilities of the base and take over as harbour authority. It has been suggested that the deep-water berth at the Coaling Pier could be used for the import of, perhaps, molasses and fertiliser, the area inside Q Pier could become a Ro-Ro ferry terminal and a marina could be established at the camber on the south-east corner of the harbour. The naval workshops can provide the facilities of a small shipyard, moreover the refrigerating capacity at the old base lends itself for use as fish storage. The tank farm to be seen on the south-west shore of the harbour is able to supply an abundance of fuel, so bunkering facilities can be available on the jetty berths.

Around the year 1860, Britain was gripped by fear of French invasion resulting in the construction of Portsmouth's heavy defences, such as the Solent forts. At the same time Portland Harbour was constructed with similar mighty defences. Four large breakwaters were made over a period of 23 years by convict labour in the 19th Century using quarried Portland stone which

Plate 124. Small craft can pass under the cable

Plate 123. South Ship Channel is blocked by the submerged HMS Hood *and a wire hawser carrying a 415V power cable.*

was unfit for masonry. There is a fort at the north end of the most easterly breakwater, with a small harbour on the west side, often locally called Chequered Fort owing to the black and white squares painted on it. It is a massively strong structure which was completed in 1875 and where fourteen 12.5 inch guns were once mounted. Of the three entrances between the breakwaters, the north and east ship channels are the normal ones to use. Not only has the South Ship Channel a steel cable supporting a live 415 volt power line across it (Plate 123), but on 4 November 1914 the old battleship *Hood* was scuttled in the entrance to act as a blockship. It was intended that she should settle on an even keel across the entrance, but in the event she capsized, leaving two metres of water over her, and gaps between the breakwaters and her bow and her stern. Small craft which can get under the wires, such as fishing boats, regularly use the South Ship Channel, generally preferring the greater overhead clearance at the south-western gap adjacent to the Inner Breakwater (Plate 124). There are rocks near the surface on the north side of the Inner Breakwater, so one should not pass too close and one should look out for divers who are often trained on the wreck. A combination of the wreck, an outgoing tide, and a stiff south-easterly can build up such a nasty sea in the entrance that it can be well worth using one of the other entrances.

There is a speed limit for power driven vessels only of 6 knots along the western shores, and a speed limit of 12 knots elsewhere in the harbour for vessels over 9 metres. Jet skis are banned within the harbour and waterskiing is not allowed close along the length of the breakwaters. There are controls on both diving and fishing mainly relating to the old naval base, the range areas and breakwater areas, and it is necessary to obtain permission from the harbourmaster before undertaking these activities. If a flying boat is operating from the harbour it is worth mentioning that whilst seaborne, the flying boat has to conform to the collision regulations like any other vessel.

Until it is closed in 1999, there remains some naval activity associated with the Naval Air Station within Portland Harbour. There is a restricted area within the harbour to the north east of the runway to protect helicopters in their final approach, and a 100m prohibition zone along the air station shore. As part of survival training, aircrew are put into inflatable dinghies either inside or outside the harbour from which they are rescued by helicopter. This may happen several times a week and is known as 'wet dinghy drill'. Inconveniently for dinghy racing, the large naval mooring buoys have been removed. *Rame Head*, the venerable Liberty Ship used by the Royal Marines for some lively ship-board training, will probably move elsewhere. Meanwhile she is surrounded by a 100m no-go area.

The north-west shore, between Bincleaves and Smallmouth, is a popular bathing beach and an active windsurfing and dinghy sailing area. There is a small pier and large sailing dinghy pontoon at Castle Cove belonging to the Castle Cove Sailing Club; and there are many shallow-water moorings offshore, belonging to the Castle Cove Sailing Club, the Royal Dorset Yacht Club and the Weymouth and Portland Cruising Association (Plate 125). In Portland Harbour mooring areas have been allocated to organisations who then sub-let mooring plots to individuals, so that moorings are only available to visitors by private treaty. There is a deep water anchorage area to seaward of the Castle Cove Sailing Club moorings. The mud holding ground is good but, as might be expected, it is a very uncomfortable anchorage in a south-easterly. The area is not without its minor hazards with the Western Ledges coming well out from the shore between Castle Cove and the northern arm of the breakwater, and a steep ledge which shows at low water on either side of the

Plate 125. Yacht moorings off Castle Cove and Sandsfoot Castle.

crumbling Sandsfoot Castle, built in Henry VIII's reign. Locals use the storm water outfall post in line with the pier to judge the position of the east end of the castle ledge, but the general rule is that the ledges can be avoided by not going inshore of the moorings. The private Castle Cove Sailing Club pier can be used by members of other sailing clubs, provided the steps are left clear of dinghies. There is another landing place to the east of Western Ledges, between the outfall pipe on the cliff and the breakwater, with a path up to Underbarn Walk.

The Weymouth Sailing Centre has been established at Sandsfoot Beach, to the west of Sandsfoot Castle at the very end of Old Castle Road. Its activities include the running of dinghy sailing and windsurfer regattas up to international level, besides teaching sailing, handling of sportsboats, windsurfing, canoeing and waterskiing for individuals or for groups.

It was not until 30 January 1839 that a bridge was constructed at Smallmouth to link Portland to Dorset by road. On the north-east side of the bridge there is a small harbour owned by the Ilchester Estate where the old entrance to the Fleet used to be. The Ferrybridge Boatyard, on the south side of the bridge, caters for yachtsmen, divers, windsurfers and indeed anyone else (Plate 126). The boatyard patent slipway can take vessels up to 12m. It has a chandlery and a good small boat slipway, but launching is tricky when the tide is running in a stiff easterly.

The approach to Smallmouth is shallow, and it is usually essential to pick up the leading marks before reaching the offshore post, which is placed slightly to the north of the channel. The upper leading mark is on the bridge. It is an orange triangle, apex down, with a green isophase light. The lower leading mark, on Fisherman's Quay, is another orange triangle, apex up, with a quick flashing green light. At chart datum there is about half a metre in the approaches to Smallmouth, but with a spring tidal range of 2.5m, quite large vessels can get to the Ferrybridge Boatyard at high water to be hauled out.

The site where Portland Speed Week competitors used to sail over Smallmouth Sand, called The Ham, is particularly popular with windsurfers and is known as Sailboard Alley. Its popularity is due to the accelerated wind and smooth water on the lee side of Chesil Beach. At the southern end of Sailboard Alley, in the shallow water off the oil tanks, there are the bones of at least one old wreck.

Moving south-east past the Naval Air Station of HMS Osprey (Plate 127), likely to be busy with noisy helicopters during the week, one arrives at Castletown, wedged between the air station on the one side and the naval base on the other. There is a yacht anchorage to the north-west of Castletown Pier, outside the

Plate 126. Smallmouth looking West. The Ferrybridge Boatyard is on the left.

Plate 127. Portland Naval Base, as was. HMS Osprey, due to close down in 1999, can be seen in front of the tank farm.

moorings on the east side of the runway approach light posts, and possibly a mooring to be had on request to any local boat owner who happens to be about (Plate 128). The best landing is at the east-facing high water slip below the castellated wall beside the castle, another of the fortifications built in Henry VIII's time, and worth a visit when it is open in summer.

Castletown Pier is commercially active with fishing boats using the west side, and stone traders and others using the remainder. There is a public beach, best used at high water, between Castletown Pier and the old naval base where many local boats are pulled up on the shore. On the west side, a dividing wall has been built to separate the public beach from the old Port Auxiliary Unit slipway. The old naval base jetties lie to the east of Castletown, protected to some extent from the prevailing wind by two sections of Mulberry Harbour breakwater, originally intended for use as artificial harbour wall for the support of D day landings in World War II.

Plate 128. The Castletown private moorings lie between the air station and the Mulberry harbour.

Chapter 10

The Fleet

The Fleet is the seven-mile shallow lagoon enclosed between Chesil Beach and the Dorset mainland. Maps divide it into the East Fleet and West Fleet, and locals call it the Little Sea. It was used during World War II for trials of Dr Barnes Wallis's bouncing bomb used in the Dambusters raid. It has been recorded as a managed centre of bird life since 1393. Today the sanctuary has legal status and is of international importance. The Fleet is currently one of the increasingly rare wetlands where wildfowl can live in peace. For example there is a winter population of up to 5,000 widgeon and brent geese, 300 red breasted merganser and goldeneye, and a handful of great northern and red throated divers at the more salty East Fleet and Portland Harbour. A number of grebe, pochard, tufted duck, pintail, teal and shoveller prefer the fresher-watered west end. As little terns and ringed plover nest on the pebble banks, Chesil Beach is closed in the breeding season between 1 May and 31 August, but access is allowed on the open sea side for the winter months. Special requests should be referred to the Chesil Bank and Fleet Nature Reserve Warden on (01305) 760579. Some plants manage to survive on the bank, such as sea kale, sea pea and yellow-horned poppy besides animals such as hares, rats, mice, shrews and voles.

Chesil is probably derived from the Saxon name 'cisel' meaning shingle. The bank is 12m above high water at the Portland end and only 6m at the Bridport end. The pebbles are sized from about 6cm at the west end, to 1.5cm opposite Abbotsbury and to 0.5cm at West Bay, indicating a grading action from east to west. The bulk of the shingle is flint, there is a good deal of white limestone, particularly to the east, and the occasional pebbles of black chert and quartz.

There is only 4.5m clearance under Smallmouth Bridge at chart datum, denying access to the Fleet to most sailing vessels. However many launches and fishing boats have moorings there. The channel is deep at the narrow point where the tide sluices in and out at three knots. To keep in the main channel, turn slightly to port after the bridge, then follow the bend round to starboard

Plate 129. The south-east end of The Fleet. Tidmoor Point is in the centre of the picture and Chickerell Hive headland is on the left.

parallel to the beach. The central sand bank is said to have a tendency to shift.

Low profile craft which can pass under the bridge may navigate past the Royal Engineers Bridging Depot to Foxhole Point, but there are restrictions on power vessels proceeding further though oars are allowed. The best way of seeing the Fleet as far as Langton Herring is to take the coastal path along the shore.

The channel is three or four metres deep under the bridge with sand banks beyond exposed at low water. The best channel guide is the line of the moorings, and in general the deeper water is found on the Chesil Beach side, where several small boatyards are to be seen. There are a good many dinghies at the promontory known as Martleaze for use as tenders to the moored craft, and opposite the camp various forms of waterborne military activity may occur. The first part of the narrows on the north side is called Monkey's Island, after a man-made refuge from where youngsters used to swim, and beyond is Locket Hole, at the Bridging Camp slipway. On the beach opposite, hollows called 'canns' form as a result of the sea working its way through and dissolving the clay base.

To the west of the narrows the Fleet becomes shallower, and for conservation reasons, only craft under oars are allowed. If exploring by rowing boat it is advisable to go up and back with the tide, following the best depth of water near Chesil Beach. Once past the holiday chalets at Wyke Regis the Fleet becomes rural, quiet and beautiful.

The blunt promontory with a rifle range on the north shore is called Tidmoor Point (Plate 129). Then comes Big Lake before the next point called Chickerell Hive (Plate 130). This is the first of several places from where flat-bottomed craft, called trows, operated in the past. They were about five metres in length, and their task was to collect and sell the catch brought by seine-net fishing boats to the seaward side of Chesil Beach. The catch was taken over the crest of the beach, called the Rudge, loaded aboard the trow, and then taken down to Ferrybridge, which in those days was called The Passage.

After Chickerell Hive, the bay near to the village of Fleet is called Butter Street Cove (Plate 131). From here the Fleet narrows to Park Wall, once another haven for trows. Next comes the Moonfleet Manor Hotel, once Fleet House. Until the war this was a private house, built possibly in 1603, for the Mohun or Moone family. Though Fleet House survived the great storm of 22 November 1824 the village of Fleet was swept away by waves which, so it was said, came right over Chesil Beach and half a mile inland. The village of Chiswell at Portland was destroyed in the same storm.

Yet further west there is little depth, and increasing amounts of eel grass. For conservation reasons there is no access by boat allowed north of the stream called Rodden Brook (Plate 132). There are notices to this effect and a black hut on Chesil Beach marks the limit as well. Nonetheless Abbotsbury Swannery is well worth a visit by road between March and the beginning of November when it is open to visitors.

Plate 130. Chickerell Hive headland is on the right and Butter Street Cove is to the left of it. The Moonfleet Manor Hotel can be seen on the extreme left where The Fleet narrows at Park Wall.

Plate 131. Butter Street Cove.

Plate 132. The north-west end of The Fleet. The Moonfleet Manor Hotel is towards the bottom and to the right and the Abbotsbury Swannery is at the far end of The Fleet on the right. Rodden Brook comes out at the third bay west from the hotel, opposite the black hut which can be seen as a speck on Chesil Beach.

Chapter 11

Portland Island

From a distance Portland Island (Plate 133) looks barren and bleak, with hardly a tree to break its dark silhouette. The distinctive wedge shape of Portland is part of the same strata forming the Gadcliff at Brandy Bay. A layer of Portland limestone lies on top of the softer layers of Portland sand and Kimmeridge clay, evident on the south-east coast of the Bill where erosion has caused impressive caves like bomb shelters. Many of London's famous buildings, such as St Paul's Cathedral, County Hall, Mansion House, The Monument, Somerset House and the Foreign Office are constructed of Portland stone. Portland stone is still quarried, and huge lumps are to be seen departing by lorry, rather than exclusively by sea as in the past.

The bare east coast of the Bill may not at first sight appear to offer much sanctuary to small craft, yet there are coves and landing places out of the tide which serve well in calm weather.

Before the Portland Harbour breakwaters were constructed from local stone at great cost and effort, Balaclava Bay was a winter haven for fishing craft, one or two of which are still pulled up on the beach. There is nothing to stop landing there now, though more attractive spots can be found. One should be aware of the existence of a patch of dangerous rocks about 50m offshore, and some wooden posts protecting an outfall pipe.

Heading south, the chart shows deep water to within 100m of the shore, as indeed is the case, but closer in there are the remains of three piers called King's Pier, Queen's Pier and Folly Pier: and odd rocks along the coast come up to the surface from five metres depth (Plate 134). The piers were built for embarking quarried stone at the time when the stone industry was flourishing. In particular Kings Pier was used for loading stone for the rebuilding of St Paul's Cathedral after the great fire of London.

The rock off Grove Point, awash at high water springs, is called Old Gardener locally, and is the site of a new sewer pipe outlet (Plate 135). For a period of seven hours or more after high water at Portland or Weymouth (they are the same) Fiddler's Race forms off Grove Point, which can be extremely choppy in a south-easterly.

Plate 133. Portland Island. The fishing boat on the east side is following the recommended route.

Plate 134. Numerous offshore rocks, some uncharted, are to be found between Balaclava Bay and Grove Point. Note the Youth Custody Centre standing on top of the cliff.

Plate 135. Little Beach lies in the centre of the photograph. Old Gardener Rock can be seen on the right, off the outfall pipe.

Around the corner there is a remote pebble bay, appropriately called Little Beach, where small birds sing and ravens swoop. It is a pleasant place which catches the morning sun, but it does have a difficult approach even for dinghies, with a bar of rocks to watch for when approaching from the point (Plate 136). The best way in is from the south, and then to land at the north end by the white flat-topped rocks .

The buildings on top of the cliff form part of the Youth Custody Centre, originally established as a prison in 1848 to provide a labour force for the construction of the harbour breakwaters. There is a splendid view from the car park on the cliff top. Nearby is Verne Fortress, a prison since 1950, where there used to be 12.5 inch guns and massive defences in the 19th Century. Beside it was the high-angle muzzle-loading gun battery. With ranges of up to four miles these guns could bring plunging fire onto the decks of vessels approaching from any direction.

Plate 136. Little Beach, viewed from the south.

Plate 137. Durdle Pier.

The next point of interest to the south of Little Beach is Durdle Pier, this being the name given to the most northerly of the cranes sited along the shore (Plate 137). Before 1924 the crane was used for loading stone, and since then for lifting open fishing boats into the sea from the cliff top. There is scarcely any depth of water under the crane at low water springs, but when the tide is up fishermen manage to launch here in up to force six winds from the west.

After rounding the headland to the south of Durdle, called Nuncle Dick's Point, one arrives at Church Ope Cove, ope being an abbreviation for open, in a navigational sense (Plate 138). The Church Ope beach used to be sandy and a major fishing cove before unwanted quarried material was tipped over nearby cliffs. Now it is composed of well-rounded rocks and shingle between Boy's Rocks on the north side of the bay, and Girl's Rocks on the

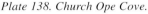

Plate 138. Church Ope Cove.

south (Plate 139). A pleasant lunch time anchorage spot on a sandy patch in three metres depth close off the beach can be found, until the sun disappears behind the cliff. There used to be a stone-loading pier at Boy's Rocks, but this was swept away in a storm in 1665. To the north of these rocks is Steamer Rock, shaped like a submarine. The ruined guard tower visible above the bay is Rufus or Bow and Arrow castle, first referred to in 1142 when it was captured by Earl Robert of Gloucester, who was known as the Red Earl. The beach at Church Ope, being the only easily accessible landing place sheltered from the prevailing wind, was the natural choice for a raid from the sea. It may be surprising to find that between 700 and 1200 years ago Portland Island was one of the richest manors in the country and thus became a target for Viking invaders who landed at Church Ope on three occasions, making off with the local girls and anything else they could find of value. Hence the need for the castle.

Plate 139. Church Ope Cove seen from seaward.

Portland Museum will be found at the top of the cliff and, amongst many exhibits, an example of a Barnes Wallis bouncing bomb. This version was an early prototype, round and dimpled like a golf ball, but the final versions were cylindrical rather than round as shown in the film, a fact that was still confidential when the film was made. The museum was founded by Dr Marie Stopes of birth control fame. For many years she owned the higher lighthouse at The Bill which she used as a holiday home and her son Harry came to marry Mary Wallis, daughter of the inventor.

Sea visitors to Church Ope may be interested to know that a useful north-going eddy runs for three hours close along the shore at Church Ope, starting one hour before low water Portland.

Plate 140. Freshwater Bay. The old pump house is on top of the square cliff.

South of Church Ope it is possible to sail close to the cliffs on the way to Freshwater Bay, locally called Neddyfield. This has become a place where rock climbers practise, and a bit of a rubbish tip. It owes its name to a freshwater spring which emerged at the bottom of the square-cornered vertical face in the cliff (Plate 140), called Red Door. The grass-covered building on top, between Cheyne House and the cliff top, was the pumping station for supplying fresh water to the naval base via an intermediate pumping station adjacent to Folly Pier.

Just to the south of Red Door, large quantities of stone have been pushed over the cliff where beforehand there was a sandy beach, and the rock leaning against the cliff on the south side of the bay is named, as one might expect when one sees it, Tank Rock.

The point on the south side of Freshwater Bay (Plate 141) is called God Nore on the chart, but the locals say that it is, and always has been, called Breston; they say that the next point south is called God Nore, known previously as Holy Point. The cliffs between the two points are called Longstone Ope, and this is the start of a dramatic piece of coastline where the soft rock under the great slab of Portland stone has become substantially eroded. Towards the south of Longstone Ope, just before God Nore in local parlance, there is a pair of cranes at a fishing boat launching point called Sandholes, situated over a cave (Plate 142). Access to the boats used to be by means of four lengths of rope with knots every half metre or so, hanging over the cliff.

Plate 141. Breston Point – as the locals call it – or God Nore, as charted.

Plate 142. Sandholes Cranes.

These have now gone and there is only a crumpled steel ladder and the ledges left to use. Well-fendered boats can get in here and find two metres of depth or more around high water. Sandholes can be used by fishing boats in worse weather than the other launching points on the east coast of The Bill, as the waves do not build up until into the cave. There is also a rough track from Sandholes to the road, best suited to four-wheel drive vehicles. God Nore Point, as the locals will have it, is just to the south of Sandholes, and is another point where a race can develop. All the races in the area, apart from Portland and Fiddler's Races, are locally called 'shaffles'.

Another huge cave appears south of the point with a stream tumbling over the centre. By keeping to the north side, a small boat can enter in about 12m. This is rather what happened to the *Reliance*, the wreck shown on the chart. Before she broke up her forepart drove right into the cave on 3 June 1949, and only the remains of the engine are now left on the seabed at the cave mouth.

Broad Ope is the name of the stretch of shore between local God Nore and The Bill, with many horizontal ledges left from stone workings. There the tide is slack for three hours either side of high water (Plate 143). There is another point, south of locals' God Nore, called Ways End with a rock just south again called 'Island'. Broad Ope also gives its name to the fishing boat crane standing over a deep cavern called Cave Hole immediately to the south of Island. From here access to the fishing boats is by means of wasted iron rungs set into the rock on the south-facing slant of cliff. It is not an easy alongside berth as there is a one metre deep shelf of rock under the ladder. Thus it may be better to stay further out in deeper water and just put a bow up to the ladder.

Proceeding south past more impressive caves towards the line of the Old Low Lighthouse and the Old High Lighthouse, a submerged reef will be encountered, called Chair Ledge, just

Plate 143. Broad Ope Crane and (locally called) God Nore Point on the right.

Plate 144. First Beach, otherwise known as Rudge Poryx, can be seen in the centre.

before a corner in the cliff where there is a beach. This is now called First Beach, though the old name for it of Rudge Poryx is still used (Plate 144). It is possible to land at the north end, under the overhang, in calm conditions, with best approach from the south. Alternatively it is possible to traverse a short stretch of water, known as River, and go alongside a ledge, at Butts Beach, just further south and actually on the line of the two old lighthouses (Plate 145). A piece of angle iron has been set into the rock, giving an easy point to secure to, and the ledge is sometimes called Metal Rock for this reason. Probably the ledge at Butts Beach was once a loading rock for the stone boats, as evidently this area provided good quality stone. The shore area at Butts is also called Red Pool after a rock pond at the back of the ledge, which sometimes turns red through lying stagnant between spring tides. It was here that the trawler *Marguerita* went ashore in a gale in 1946 with the loss of her Danish crew, and at low water spring tide bits of wreck can be seen from the cliff.

Plate 145. Butts Beach and the old lighthouses from seaward. Metal Rock is on the left.

Plate 146. Collars Ledge on the right, and Robinson Crusoe Island in the centre.

The next ledge, with no easy landing, is called Long Points which, as its name implies, has submerged extensions. After that comes Collar's Ledge lying due south of the Old Low Lighthouse which has good landing places on both sides at mid-tide, though nothing at all to tie up to (Plate 146). The flat-topped island to the south is called Robinson Crusoe Island, and the beach behind is called Pom Pom.

The most southerly of the fishing boat derricks, which fishermen have been using since 1873, called Red Crane (Plate 147) stands on the next promontory. There are two or three metres under the crane jib at high water, a smooth alongside position, shaped to take a boat, and access by a chain hanging from the cliff with adjacent foot holes. The flat ledge called Mugley's Plain (Plate 148) to the south of Red Crane ends at a gap in the rock called Boathaul, where long ago some sort of

Plate 147. Red Crane.

Plate 148. The eastern tip of Portland Island, looking north. The first five promontories, from south to north, are Mugleys Plain, Red Crane, Collars Ledge, Long Points and Iron Rock.

boathaul system once operated. There is a narrow beach at the end of Boathaul where the slightest swell will build up and break.

If rounding The Bill really close, the outermost drying rock to be encountered is in line with the present lighthouse and the 18m high Trinity house obelisk, erected in 1844, on 020°Mag (Plate 149). This was the rock that surprised a number of competitors in the ill-fated 1979 Fastnet race. When the top window of the lighthouse is in view above the obelisk from an open boat one is clear of the rock.

About one third of the distance along the south-west facing shore of The Bill there are a number of rocks, amongst them one

Plate 149. The tip of Portland Bill.

once called The Snail. Through natural erosion this rock has lost its identity and now gives its name to the shore between The Bill and Pulpit Rock (Plate 150). There is deep water close to Pulpit Rock, but even so due regard should be paid to the south-going Lyme Bay tidal stream which fairly sizzles past at times. Both the tip of The Bill and the area round the corner provided the stone for the government buildings of Whitehall in London; hence the local name Whitehall for the 200m stretch of coast to the north of Pulpit Rock.

There is a radio beacon at Portland Bill Lighthouse, transmitting PB on a frequency of 291.9kHz. The principal light flashes through most of the visible arc four times every twenty seconds, but there is a reducing number of flashes in sectors marked on the chart at either side of The Bill. The red sector light showing over the Shambles comes from the lowest lighthouse

Plate 150. Pulpit Rock.

window on the east side and not the main light. Portland Bill Lighthouse is due south (True) of the Old High Lighthouse. The derelict old Coastguard lookout station has been refurbished by the National Coastwatch Institution with the intention of manning it again in future.

The Admiralty chart of 1863 describes the Portland Race as 'a periodical commotion of the sea which rages with great violence'. Even if it cannot be seen in darkness or fog, it can be heard some miles away - as Adlard Coles put it - 'like the rumble of a distant train'. It must be said that Portland Race should be treated seriously, and on many occasions the only wise choice is to pass between two and five miles to the south of The Bill, depending upon the severity of the weather. The Race is formed by strong Channel tides running over a dramatically steep ledge containing caverns as big as a cathedral, so divers say, and strong cross-currents running south for nine hours out of twelve on either side of The Bill. The Race moves, as one would expect, from one side of the ledge to the other dependent upon the direction of the Channel stream. The most dangerous seas occur, as might also be expected, with spring tides and southerly winds. Worst of all, so the most experienced fishermen say, is the combination of a south-easterly gale with a spring ebb tide. In such conditions, coming from Weymouth, it will be advisable to leave the Shambles to starboard and take a course five miles south of The Bill.

In more moderate conditions The Race is obviously still to be avoided. Although a well-found and skilfully handled boat is unlikely to sink if caught up in it, there is always a danger of losing someone overboard. The best course of action within The Race is to attach safety harnesses to something really solid, close all hatches and point down the seas at the minimum speed to ensure steerage way. The tide, which may be running at seven knots or more, will carry a vessel through The Race in about ten unforgettable minutes.

The inshore passage gives a channel clear of The Race up to a mile wide at times (Plate 151). No matter what the state of wind and tide, there is always some sort of gap between the shore and The Race, which is narrowest at the start of the Channel flood tide. However when a south-easterly combines with a spring ebb tide, white water between The Race and The Bill gives the appearance of The Race having closed the inshore passage.

Plate 151. Portland Bill and The Race. Note the calmer water off The Bill and on either side.

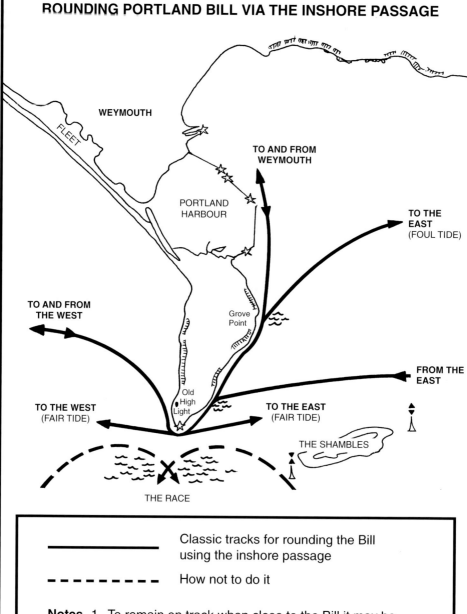

ROUNDING PORTLAND BILL VIA THE INSHORE PASSAGE

WEYMOUTH

FLEET

TO AND FROM
WEYMOUTH

PORTLAND
HARBOUR

TO THE
EAST
(FOUL TIDE)

TO AND FROM
THE WEST

Grove
Point

FROM THE
EAST

TO THE WEST
(FAIR TIDE)

Old
High
Light

TO THE EAST
(FAIR TIDE)

THE SHAMBLES

THE RACE

―――――― Classic tracks for rounding the Bill
using the inshore passage

- - - - - - How not to do it

Notes 1. To remain on track when close to the Bill it may be
necessary to steer well to the north.
2. When the tide is fair it is not necessary to make to the
north after rounding the Bill.

Plate 152. Rounding The Bill via the inshore passage.

Given reasonable weather conditions, westward-going vessels taking the inshore passage should do so in the period four hours after high water Portland to two hours before high water Portland; and eastward-going vessels should take it two hours before high water Portland to four hours after high water Portland (Plate 152). Thus, for example, by leaving Weymouth two or three hours after high water, a vessel heading west will have the benefit of the stream down the east coast of The Bill, and then the full favourable Channel ebb tide. Locals say that when making to the west, favourable rounding conditions occur as soon as Collars Ledge (see Plate 146) uncovers after high water. In fact the inshore passage at any state of the tide will seldom cause a problem to an experienced crew in reasonable weather, in daylight and with a well-found boat capable of 7 knots under engine. For example, fishing boats seldom go outside the race at any state of the tide when it is more convenient to use the inshore passage. Even so, power-driven vessels are at risk of fouling a propeller with a lobster pot line when the marker buoy has been dragged below the surface by the current. As the stream runs south on both sides of The Bill it is unlikely that a disabled craft would end up on the rocks. Nevertheless, when caught in the slacker tides near The Bill, disabled vessels have been driven ashore by a southerly wind.

A vital point to remember is that the tidal stream runs southwards on both sides of the island for most of the tidal cycle. Thus the approach to the inshore passage should be from well to the north of The Bill. Approaching the inshore passage from the east against a contrary Channel tide, it will pay to steer a mile

127

north of The Shambles, then pick up the south-going stream - they call it the Southern - off Breston (God Nore). Even when the Channel tide is favourable, it is best to approach the Bill from north of the Shambles to avoid being carried into the race, though powerful craft do manage to avoid it by motoring hard to the north-north-west from the west Shambles Buoy. The Bill should be rounded at 200m distance to stay in the slack water off The Snail as long as possible, before arriving at the strong south-going stream off Pulpit Rock - they call this the Flood.

Having passed Pulpit Rock one must check ones progress to the north. If it becomes clear after a minute or two that even when past the worst of the tide off Pulpit Rock, there is still insufficient boat speed to get over the tide, the best plan is to turn round, go back into the tidal lee off the Bill and wait for the tide to ease. On the other hand, given enough boat speed to get over the tide, one will find the strength of the stream lessens if one allows one's craft to be gradually set out to the west. She will start to make more and more favourable progress to the north-west and eventually break clear of the south-going stream into the more tranquil waters of Lyme Bay.

If approaching the tip of The Bill from the south-west in a late attempt to take the inshore passage when the Flood is running down the west side of The Bill, it is almost inevitable that a vessel will end up in the race. A celebrated occasion when this happened was during the passage of the Spanish Armada up the English Channel. The Spanish Commander in Chief, the Duke of Medina Sidonia, had despatched four galeasses, vessels using sails and oars, to deal with Frobisher's ships which had been seen anchored, possibly becalmed, off The Bill. But the galeasses were no match for The Race and were forced to retire in grand confusion. Thus steering from west to east, a course should be taken to bring one no further south than the Old High Lighthouse, and from there, the coast should be followed at 200m distance round The Bill and all the way to Grove Point. By hugging the shore the worst of the south-going set will be avoided as well as the broken water further offshore. It should be mentioned that, under certain conditions such as a south-easterly gale, Fiddler's Race off Grove Point and the race off Godnore can be almost as bad as Portland Race itself. Fiddler's Race cannot be altogether avoided by taking a route close inshore and care should be taken to avoid Gardener's Rock. It should also be remembered that the inshore route, while clearly more safe and comfortable in a westerly wind, is hazardous in an easterly wind with a lee shore so close.

In conclusion, the Shambles should be mentioned as a curious shingle and broken shell bank two miles to the east of the Bill. It would seem logical to assume that the Shambles might form in the centre of a Weymouth Bay tidal whirlpool, but this does not happen, and it is a mystery why this shingle-upon-clay bank should remain in such a strong tidal stream. Incidentally the direction and strength of the current at the west Shambles buoy conforms with the Channel stream, and is not influenced by the Portland peninsula. In calm weather fishing boats will often be seen over the bank but since there is less than 4 metres charted depth, seas can break heavily on the Shambles, to create a very dangerous area for both large and small craft. Ships have been wrecked on the Shambles from time to time: for example, the duty coastguard observed a brig with painted gun ports running onto the Shambles on 11 August 1852. There were no survivors and the brig was never identified.

There used to be a light ship at the east end, but whilst the Shambles is now clearly marked with buoys, it is quite easy to confuse the east buoy with west or vice-versa.

Chapter 12

Military Activities between
St Aldhelm's Head and Portland Bill

The Lulworth Ranges

The Armoured Fighting Vehicle Gunnery School uses the Lulworth ranges for gunnery training for British Army armoured vehicles through most of the year, night and day. Live as well as practice ammunition is fired, and big tanks such as the Challenger discharge large calibre high-velocity shells of formidable might (Plate 153). The principal activity takes place on weekdays at the Bindon range to the north of the Purbeck Downs, so not much gets beyond the 200m high natural chalk barrier. Nevertheless a small number of the 70,000 rounds fired each year ricochet out to sea or end up on the beach. They could be high explosive, armour-piercing, phosphorus or inert.

There are two offshore zones to know about, the inner and outer sea danger areas. The inner sea danger area is the predominant one in use, extending nearly six miles offshore. The outer sea danger area, which may be used 60 times a year, extends 12 miles out. Two weeks notice is given before the outer area is used for armour-piercing fin-stabilised shells fired from the Challenger tank or Royal Artillery weapons. The outer area may be used at night and is used on six weekends during the year.

On land there is another large prohibited area when firing is taking place. This is a region of quite outstanding beauty enhanced by the fact that no new buildings have been put up for

Plate 153. A Challenger tank firing at the Lulworth Range.

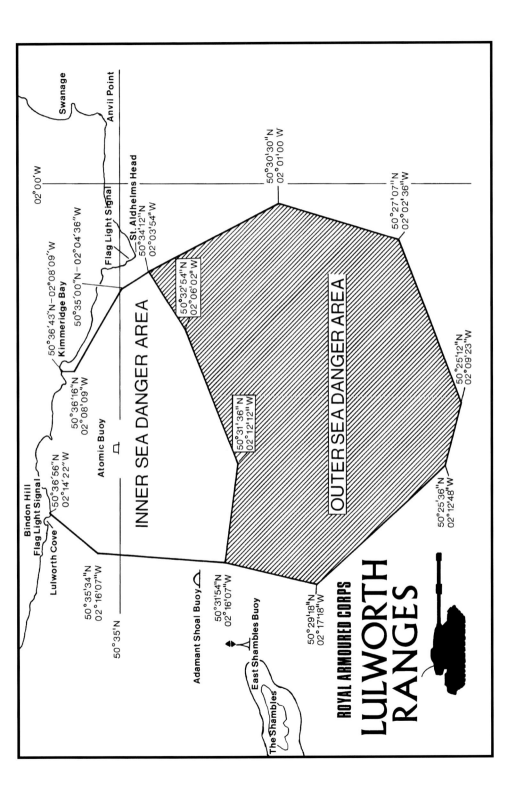

ROYAL ARMOURED CORPS
LULWORTH RANGES

INNER SEA DANGER AREA

OUTER SEA DANGER AREA

Swanage

Anvil Point

02°00'W

Flag Light Signal

St. Aldhelms Head
50°34'12''N
02°03'54''W

50°30'30''N
02°01'00''W

50°36'43''N – 02°08'09''W
Kimmeridge Bay
50°35'00''N – 02°04'36''W

50°32'54''N
02°06'02''W

50°27'07''N
02°02'36''W

50°36'16''N
02°08'09''W
Atomic Buoy

50°31'36''N
02°12'12''W

50°25'12''N
02°09'23''W

Bindon Hill
Flag Light Signal
Lulworth Cove
50°36'56''N
02°14'22''W

50°35'34''N
02°16'07''W

50°35'N

50°25'36''N
02°12'48''W

Adamant Shoal Buoy
50°31'54''N
02°16'07''W

East Shambles Buoy

50°29'18''N
02°17'18''W

The Shambles

over 50 years. In addition, owing to the absence of continuous human activity and pesticides, wildlife has prospered with unusual freedom. It makes a delightful place to visit when this is allowed but, needless to say, strange objects which might be unexploded munitions should be left severely alone.

Currently the range safety vessels are three dark blue 15m Talisman class launches (Plate 154). They do 20 knots and patrol the sea danger areas in all but extreme weather, either from their base in Portland or from fair-weather moorings at Chapman's Pool and Lulworth Cove. A similar range safety vessel was wrecked just outside Chapmans Pool on 15 December 1992. It seems that she left her mooring off Lulworth in the dark and then accidentally headed north-east rather than south-west as intended. After the accident the mooring buoy was moved further to seaward. The range safety craft, which operate on VHF Channel 8, cannot prevent vessels from crossing the ranges on passage but, acting under Ministry of Defence byelaw of 1978 No 1663, can, and do, prevent loitering. In practice there is something to be said for avoiding the relevant danger area when firing is taking place, as apart from avoiding frustration to the army going about their business, there is only a limited quota of ammunition available for any one firing period, and once this is used the restricted areas are opened, sometimes well before the scheduled time.

The daily firing times are broadcast on Radio Solent and Two Counties Radio at 7.50 and 8.50 am on weekdays. They are also given out on Radio Wessex and sometimes on Radio Dorset. Fortnightly firing programmes are sent to the coastguards and larger nearby yacht clubs; therefore it is worth making a copy of

Plate 154. The Lulworth range safety vessels berthed at the old naval base

this if cruising in the area. Alternatively one can call up the Portland Coastguard to obtain details or, when the ranges are active, get information from the range safety vessels on VHF Channel 8, or direct from the range officer on Tel (01929) 462721 extension 4819, or range control on extension 4859.

While firing is in progress, red flags and red flashing lights are displayed from St Aldhelm's Head and from Bindon Hill. Other red flags marking the inland range boundaries fly all the time and can be ignored by those at sea.

Whilst most firing on the range takes place Monday - Thursday, 9.30am - 5pm, and on Fridays, 9.30am - Noon, night firing also takes place about every fortnight, usually on Tuesdays and Thursdays. On these occasions firing will start when it gets dark, and may go on for 3-4 hours. There are six weekends allocated for territorial unit training and this includes night firing.

During holiday periods such as Easter, bank holiday weekends, Christmas and the whole of August there is no firing and this is obviously the best time to visit the range area.

Naval Activities Outside Portland Harbour

With the closure of the naval base at Portland and the move of naval operational sea training to Plymouth, naval activity off the Dorset coast is much diminished. The coastline is, however, still within designated naval exercise areas.

The helicopter air station, HMS Osprey, will remain open until 1999 and warships may continue to use the noise range off Balaclava Bay and the electronic warfare calibration range. The Naval Firing Range between the Adamant Shoal buoy and St Aldhelm's Head may be used very occasionally. The de-gaussing range is still laid to the north-east of the Portland Harbour breakwater and in the North Ship Channel. Both the noise and de-gaussing ranges use seabed sensors to measure a ship's acoustic and magnetic characteristics and ships using the range will be seen passing between yellow marker buoys flying flags PP. The 'no anchoring' areas are marked on the chart. The ranges are now owned and run by the Sea Capabilities Division of the Defence Test & Evaluation Organisation, a part of the Defence Evaluation & Research Agency (DERA), the company which has taken over scientific work from the Ministry of Defence. At the time of writing their policy regarding the future of the Portland ranges has not been made known. Another branch of the DERA, part of the Defence Research Agency based at Bincleaves, may also undertake submersible trials - such as remotely operated underwater vehicles or torpedoes - off the breakwater. The launching point is at the grey building in the centre of the north-eastern breakwater and the range extends in a direction 098°Mag for 5000m. Safety craft carrying red flags patrol the area on the occasions the range is in use, and another red flag is hoisted at the launching point.

The Naval Firing Range may still be used if the new naval range off Dodman Point is unavailable, although this is likely to be a rare event. The yellow danger zone buoys two miles off St Aldhelm's Head are used in daylight as targets for live rounds. On such occasions, anti-aircraft shells fitted with proximity fuses may be seen detonating with a big flash above sea level; or yet more spectacular high-explosive shells can be used, that create a loud report and raise a good plume of water. In order not to destroy the buoys, these shells may be fired at a flare dropped in the position bearing 096°Mag, range 13 miles, from Portland Bill Light. The shells will have been fired from ships flying a red flag going north-south up and down the five mile firing line beside the Adamant Shoal buoy. Warships may proceed up and down the firing line solely to calibrate instruments, when no red flag will be seen and there is no requirement to keep clear of the range. The Lulworth range safety vessels may act as range safety vessels when the naval range is in use. On these occasions a spotter will either be in a helicopter or on the top of St Aldhelm's Head. Firing will not take place if a vessel is within 2000m of the target.

Naval activities for the day in and around Portland are broadcast at 0830 daily on channel 13. This is preceded by warning calls on channels 6,8,10 and 16.

Plate 155. The Adamant Shoal buoy.

Appendix I

Tidal Stream Charts between Portland and St Aldhelm's Head.

Appendix II

Tidal Stream Charts between Durlston Bay and Handfast Point.

The following tidal stream charts have been prepared after consultation with authoritative local fishermen.

It is appreciated that these tidal streams differ from conventional wisdom. Nevertheless the author has found that those who have spent a lifetime working lobster pots, at one time under sail and oar, know the inshore tides best. After all, such knowledge is essential for managing a number of pots efficiently, especially as some floats only surface at slack water.

Before World War II the Weymouth Sailing Club obtained tidal stream information from one of the same sources, and these have stood the test of time.

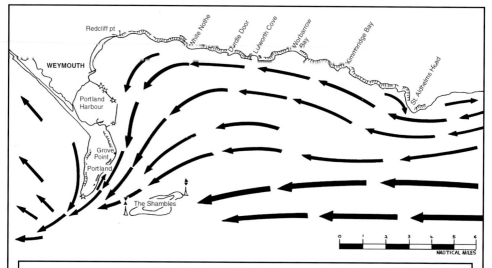

SIX HOURS BEFORE HIGH WATER WEYMOUTH

Main Channel west-going stream stronger than inshore stream.

Portland and St Aldhelm's Head races strong. South-going stream on both sides of The Bill.

North-going eddy off Church Ope.

Tidal level at Portland and Weymouth will stand near low water level for a further four hours at spring tides. After low water neaps the tide rises for three hours, then stands for two, before rising again.

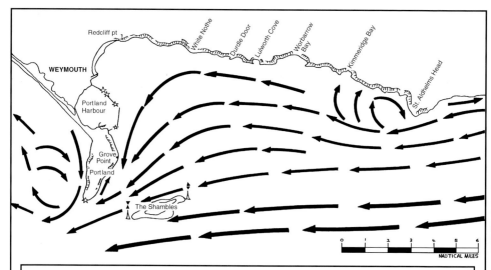

FIVE HOURS BEFORE HIGH WATER WEYMOUTH

Channel stream flowing strongly to the west.

South-going streams on both sides of The Bill, and circular streams on the west side of the Bill and St Aldhelm's Head.

North-going eddy off Church Ope.

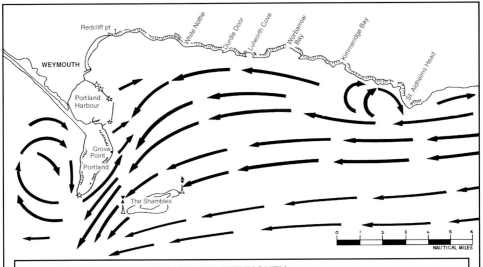

FOUR HOURS BEFORE HIGH WATER WEYMOUTH

Channel stream becoming less strong.
Circular stream on the west side of The Bill and St Aldhelm's Head.
Easterly inshore stream developing between Portland Bill and Anvil Point.
Inshore streams slack at neap tides between Grove Point and God Nore.

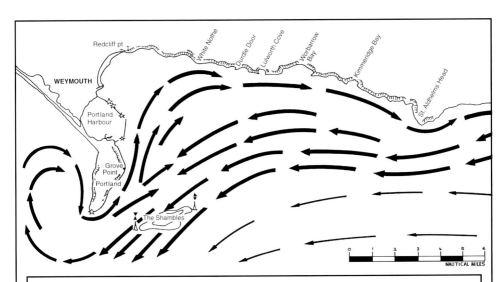

THREE HOURS BEFORE HIGH WATER WEYMOUTH

West-going Channel stream weak.
Circular stream on the west side of The Bill with strong south- going component.
Inshore easterly stream from Portland Bill to Handfast Point becoming stronger.
Stream off the east side of The Bill flowing south-west.
Portland and St Aldhelm's Race easing.

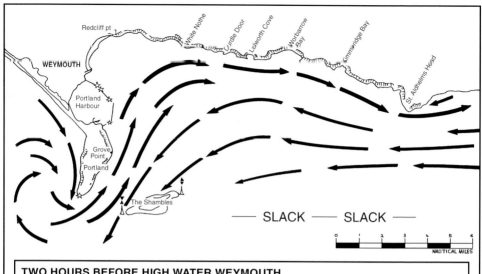

TWO HOURS BEFORE HIGH WATER WEYMOUTH

Channel stream slack.
Inshore stream flowing strongly north-east to east.
Stream further out - i.e. 3-4 miles offshore - flowing south-west to west.
Circular stream on west side of Portland Bill with strong south-going component.
West-going inshore stream at Winspit.

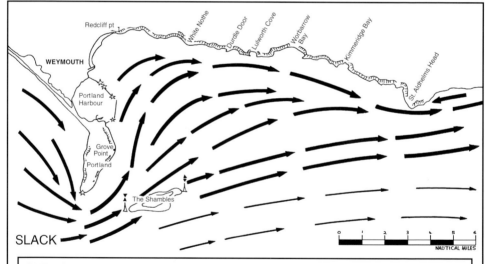

ONE HOUR BEFORE HIGH WATER WEYMOUTH

Inshore stream stronger than the Channel stream.
Strong south-going stream on the west side of The Bill.
Slack water to the south-west of The Bill.

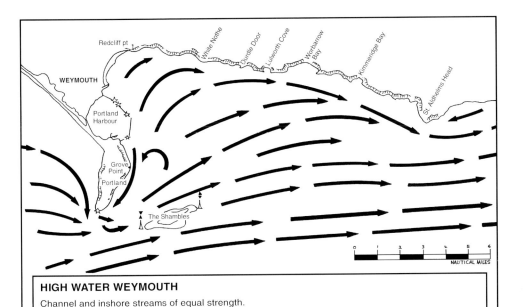

HIGH WATER WEYMOUTH

Channel and inshore streams of equal strength.
Strong south-going streams on both sides of The Bill.
Portland and St Aldhelm's Races strong.
Anti-clockwise circular tide off Grove Point.

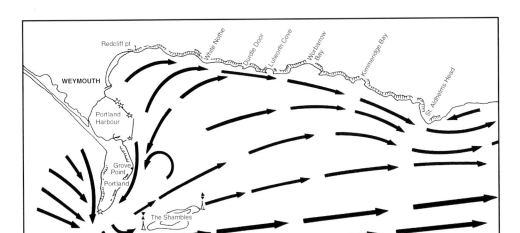

ONE HOUR AFTER HIGH WATER WEYMOUTH

Channel stream stronger than inshore stream.
South-going streams on both sides of The Bill.
Portland and St Aldhelm's Races strong.
Circular tide on the east side of The Bill.

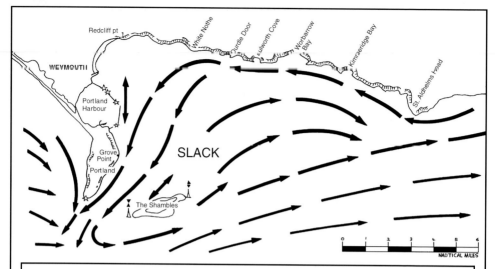

TWO HOURS AFTER HIGH WATER WEYMOUTH

Main Channel stream east-going and becoming less strong.
Inshore west-going stream flowing within a half mile of the shore as far as White Nothe where it breaks off to the south- west and broadens.
South-going stream on both sides of The Bill.
Portland and St Aldhelm's Races strong.

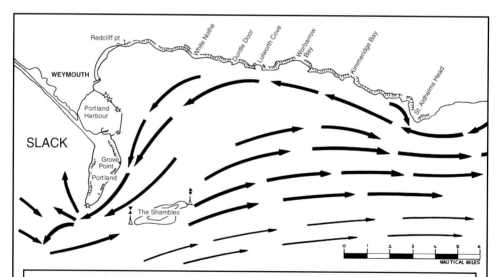

THREE HOURS AFTER HIGHWATER WEYMOUTH

East-going Channel stream weakening.
Strong inshore stream from Poole to Portland flowing westward.
Brief period of slack water between The Bill and Portland Race.
South-going eddy on west side of St Aldhelm's Head.

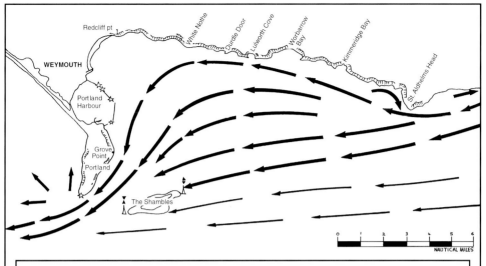

FOUR HOURS AFTER HIGH WATER WEYMOUTH

Channel stream weak west-going, or slack.
Inshore west-going stream running strongly.
North-going stream under the west side of The Bill.
East-going eddy formed to the west of Anvil point and St Aldhelm's Head.

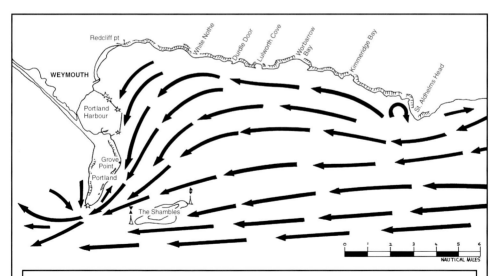

FIVE HOURS AFTER HIGH WATER WEYMOUTH

Inshore and Channel streams of equal strength.
South-going stream on west side of The Bill.
Portland and St Aldhelm's Races becoming strong.
North-going eddy forming off Church Ope.
Circular stream to the west of St Aldhelm's Head.

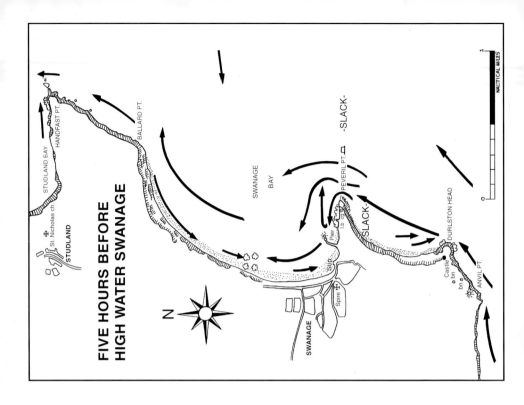

FIVE HOURS BEFORE
HIGH WATER SWANAGE

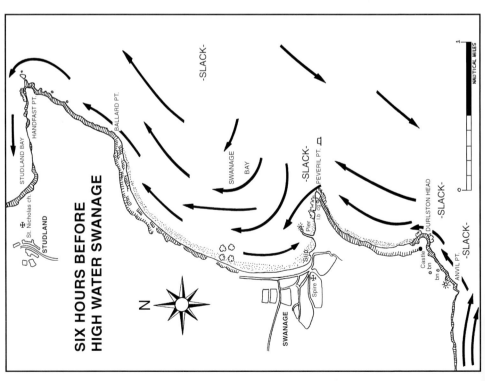

SIX HOURS BEFORE
HIGH WATER SWANAGE

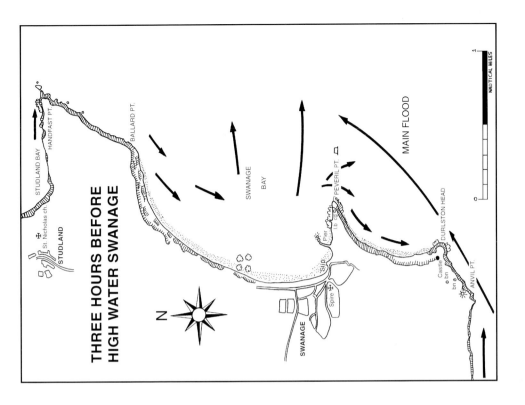

THREE HOURS BEFORE HIGH WATER SWANAGE

MAIN FLOOD

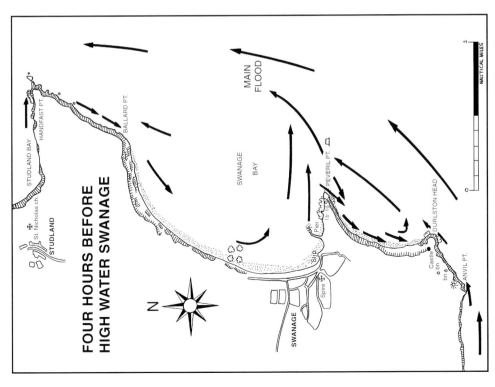

FOUR HOURS BEFORE HIGH WATER SWANAGE

MAIN FLOOD

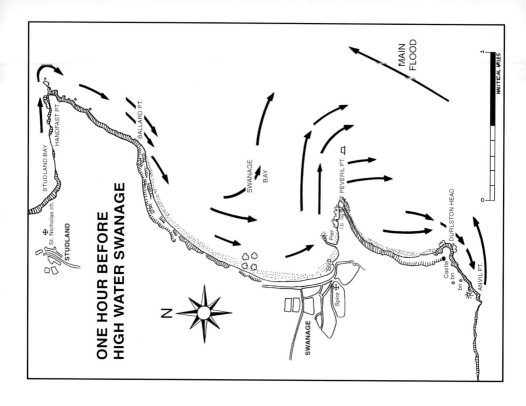

ONE HOUR BEFORE HIGH WATER SWANAGE

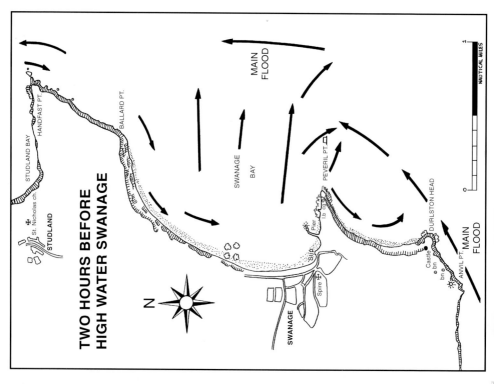

TWO HOURS BEFORE HIGH WATER SWANAGE

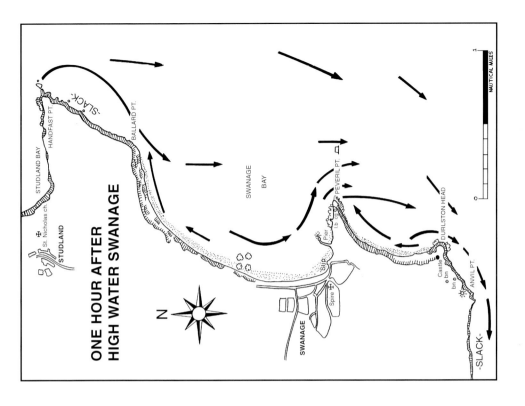

ONE HOUR AFTER HIGH WATER SWANAGE

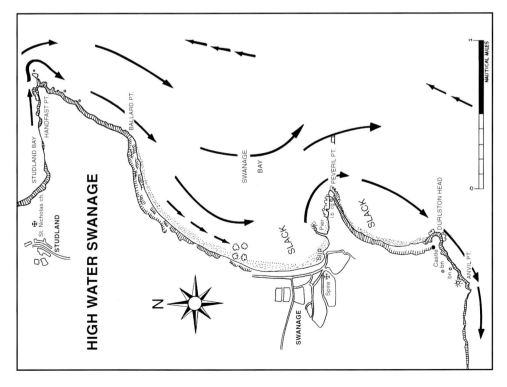

HIGH WATER SWANAGE

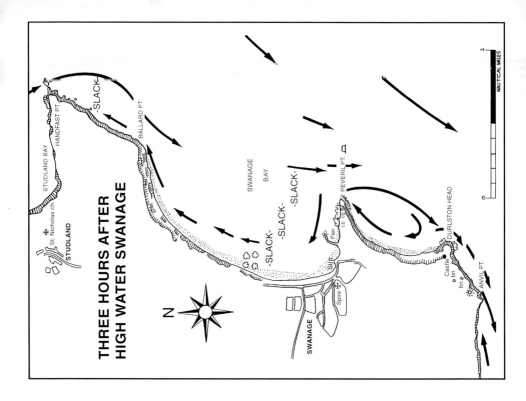

THREE HOURS AFTER HIGH WATER SWANAGE

N

STUDLAND BAY
HANDFAST PT.
St. Nicholas ch.
STUDLAND
-SLACK-
BALLARD PT.
SWANAGE
BAY
-SLACK-
-SLACK-
-SLACK-
Pier
l.b
PEVERIL PT.
Slip
Spire
Castle
bn
bn
DURLSTON HEAD
SWANAGE
ANVIL PT.

1
NAUTICAL MILES
0

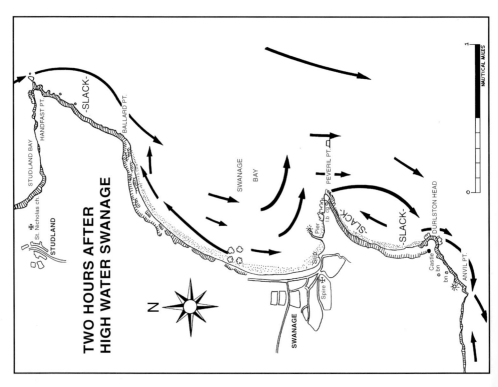

TWO HOURS AFTER HIGH WATER SWANAGE

N

STUDLAND BAY
HANDFAST PT.
St. Nicholas ch.
STUDLAND
-SLACK-
BALLARD PT.
SWANAGE
BAY
Pier
l.b
PEVERIL PT.
Slip
-SLACK-
-SLACK-
Spire
Castle
bn
bn
DURLSTON HEAD
SWANAGE
ANVIL PT.

1
NAUTICAL MILES
0

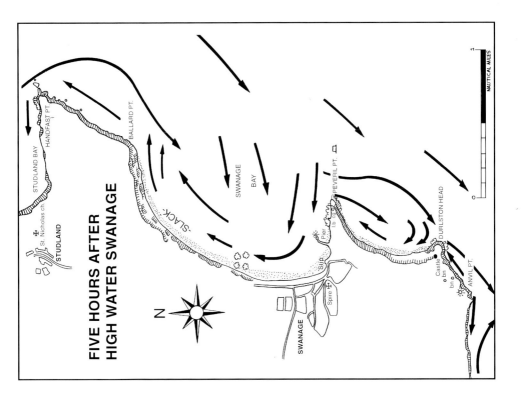

FIVE HOURS AFTER HIGH WATER SWANAGE

STUDLAND BAY

St. Nicholas ch.
STUDLAND

HANDFAST PT.

BALLARD PT.

SWANAGE BAY

-SLACK-

SWANAGE

Spire

Slip

Pier

PEVERIL PT.

Castle
bn

DURLSTON HEAD

ANVIL PT.

N

NAUTICAL MILES

0   1

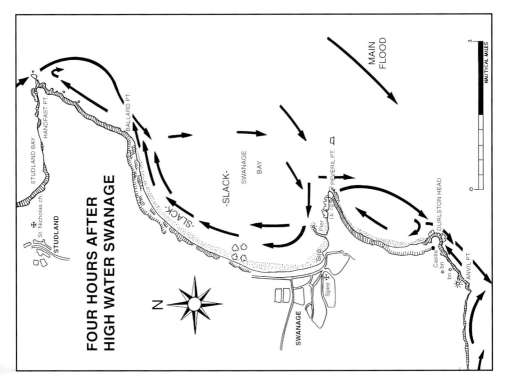

FOUR HOURS AFTER HIGH WATER SWANAGE

STUDLAND BAY

St. Nicholas ch.
STUDLAND

HANDFAST PT.

BALLARD PT.

SWANAGE BAY

-SLACK-

-SLACK-

MAIN FLOOD

SWANAGE

Spire

Slip

Pier

PEVERIL PT.

Castle
bn

DURLSTON HEAD

ANVIL PT.

N

NAUTICAL MILES

0   1

ALONG THE DORSET COAST

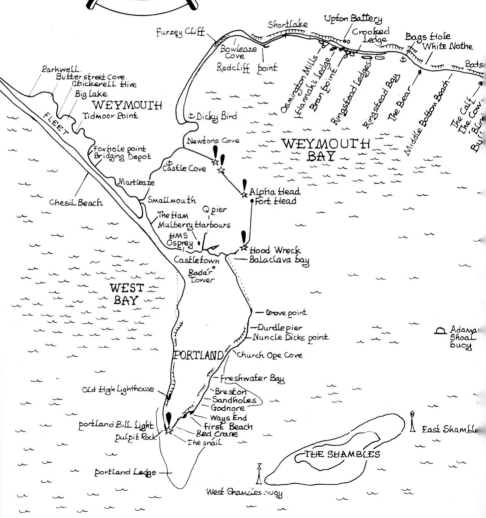

Parkwell.
Butter street Cove.
Chickerell Hive
Big Lake
WEYMOUTH
Tidmoor Point

Furzey Cliff
Bowleaze Cove
Redcliff Point
Shortlake
Upton Battery
Crooked Ledge
Bags Hole
White Nothe
Osmington Mills
Hannah's Ledge
Bran Point
Ringstead Ledges
Ringstead Bay
The Bear
Middle Bottom Beach
The Calf
The Cow
Bats
Bun

FLEET

Foxhole Point
Bridging Depot

Martleaze

Chesil Beach

Dicky Bird

Newtons Cove

Castle Cove

Smallmouth

The Ham
Mulberry Harbours
HMS Osprey

Castletown

Radar Tower

WEYMOUTH BAY

Q pier

Alpha Head
Fort Head

Hood Wreck
Balaclava Bay

WEST BAY

Grove Point
Durdle Pier
Nuncle Dicks Point
Church Ope Cove

PORTLAND

Freshwater Bay

Old High Lighthouse

Breston
Sandholes
Godnore
Ways End
First Beach
Red Crane
The Snail

Portland Bill Light
Pulpit Rock

Portland Ledge

Adam Shoal Buoy

East Shamble

THE SHAMBLES

West Shambles Buoy